The Devil Is Afraid of Me

The Devil Is Afraid of Me

The Life and Work of the
World's Most Famous Exorcist

by Gabriele Amorth
and Marcello Stanzione

Translated by
Charlotte J. Fasi

SOPHIA INSTITUTE PRESS
Manchester, New Hampshire

Sophia Institute Press
Box 5284, Manchester, NH 03108
1-800-888-9344

www.SophiaInstitute.com

Sophia Institute Press® is a registered trademark of Sophia Institute.

Paperback ISBN 978-1-622826-247
eBook ISBN 978-1-622826-254
Library of Congress Control Number:2019954897

5th printing

To Our Lady, Queen of the Apostles

In memoriam,
Father Clement An-Or
1982–2018
(Catholic Diocese of Katsina-Ala
Benue State, Nigeria)

—CJF

Contents

Appendices

Preface

by Piero Mantero

In a flash, the news of Father Gabriele Amorth's passing made the rounds of all the print and mass media. I cannot conceal my sorrow for such a palpable loss. I shall no longer receive his brief notes and recommendations. Among his habits was his penchant for directing authors to our editorial staff—in particular, to me, his friend. Then I would evaluate the works and do whatever was necessary to publish them.

So, naturally, my first inspiration was to seek a priest who could coauthor a small book *in memoriam* to keep in our catalogue long term; then everyone, even in posterity, would know this inspired communicator exorcist. I immediately thought of dear Don Marcello Stanzione, a prolific writer, angelologist, and admirer of Father Amorth; and he did not have to think twice about it.

For this, I thank him with all my heart; and I appeal to all those who read this work to enrich it with information and anecdotes or anything else that helps us to feel closer to our dearest Gabriele Amorth! Thank you!

The Devil Is Afraid of Me

Exorcist Par Excellence
by Marcello Stanzione

Who Father Amorth Was

In the weekly *Credere* (Believe), Francesco Bamonte, president of the International Association of Catholic Exorcists, reported the death of the Catholic Church's most famous exorcist of our times:

> Friday, September 16 at 7:37 p.m., our dearest Father Gabriele Amorth concluded his earthly journey. We recall him with the deepest gratitude for all that he has done to promote the ministry of exorcism in the contemporary Church, and we admire him for the love and affection he always demonstrated toward the persons he assisted. For nearly thirty years, he strove to relieve the sufferings of so many brothers and sisters who were the victims of the extraordinary actions of Satan, freeing them from the chains of diabolical possession through prayers of healing and liberation and exorcisms.
>
> Our association owes him much for his tireless engagement and his determined will to accompany us unsparingly. As president of the International Association of Exorcists, I had permission from his superiors to visit

him periodically during his illness. I always spoke to him of your affectionate concern and the numerous greetings that you sent him. We continue to remember him daily in our prayers, aware that he now prays for us in the peace and joy of the just. Through God's grace, he helps us to welcome God's loving plan for each one of us in this Association, which he founded and presided over as the first president, and then as an honorary member up until the very end. With the help of divine grace, we proceed with the work he initiated and fervently promoted. [With the help of his prayers,] may we continue to sustain effectively the good battle against Satan and all the other rebel angels, for the coming of God's kingdom. May we always emulate his filial and tender devotion to the Virgin Mary and bring his uplifting example to others.

Who was Father Amorth, and what was the secret of his priestly vocation?

In a 2015 interview in *Credere*, he revealed: "My vocation was born early, around the age of ten or twelve. I was more or less Jesus' age when he was found in the temple. One day, when all the family was at the table — my two saintly parents, my four brothers, and I — Papa asked us: 'What do you wish to do when you are grown up?' I responded first: 'I will be a priest.' And he said, nearly as if he expected it: 'I shall be very content if it happens.'" Papa Mario did not live to see his son a priest; he died in 1939, at the start of World War II.

Father Amorth's vocational pursuit knew many stages. One significant stage brought him to San Giovanni Rotondo to meet Padre Pio. He told *Credere*: "I went to him in 1942, a little before going to Father Alberione in Rome. I wished to have some insight on my vocation, but Padre Pio, after a long wait, gave me such an evasive response that I cannot even remember it. Nevertheless, I continued to visit him each year for twenty-six years and much to my advantage."

With Father Giacomo Alberione, things went differently. In the summer of 1942, at the age of seventeen and at the height of the war, Amorth went to Rome, accompanied by his pastor, to visit some religious institutions. He first knocked on the door of the Passionists but, because of a misunderstanding, was not received. He then visited the Roman offices of the Society of St. Paul and was welcomed personally by Blessed Giacomo Alberione, who immediately recognized his Pauline vocation. "When I asked him which order I should choose, he said: 'Tomorrow I shall celebrate a Mass for you and I shall ask the Lord.' The next day he told me: 'It is God's will that you enter the Society of St. Paul.' So I decided to finish my classical studies at the high school and then enter the Society of St. Paul."

The funeral of Father Amorth was held in the great church of the Queen of the Apostles in the neighborhood of St. Paul. The celebrants were the auxiliary bishop Monsignor Paolo Lojudice and the superior general of the Society of St. Paul, Father Valdir José de Castro. There were a hundred priests concelebrating with them, among whom were numerous exorcists and the president of their international organization, Father Francesco Bamonte. At least fifteen hundred people attended the funeral; those not able to enter the church remained in the churchyard. At least a thousand people also waited all day Sunday and then Monday morning to file past the casket that was placed in the church next to the tomb of Blessed Giacomo Alberione, the founder of the Society of St. Paul. People who had experienced Father Gabriele's comfort and help in their illnesses came from all over Italy and beyond. Many of the participants of the numerous prayer groups that Father Gabriele followed in Rome were also there, as were the many that joined him in prayer for the exorcisms.

As a Pauline priest, Father Amorth fully lived his vocation as an apostle of communication from 1985 until his death. As a publicist, he promoted a deeper knowledge of the world of the occult and its remedies in the Church. As a molder of the young Pauline seminarians, he taught at the high school and was a spiritual director for diverse institutions (the Little Sisters of the Annunciation, the Gabrielines, and the members of the Institute of Jesus the Priest); and briefly, for a little less than two years, he was the Paulines' delegate for Italy. Moreover, thanks to his wise pen, he was an appreciated journalist and editorialist. From 1980 to 1988, he directed the monthly *Madre di Dio* (Mother of God) and collaborated with the editors of *Credere, Famiglia cristiana* (The Christian family), *Segno del soprannaturale* (The sign of the supernatural), and other Pauline magazines. Then, for many long years, each second Wednesday of the month, he hosted the series *An Exorcist Tells His Story* on Radio Maria.

He became very well known internationally thanks to his books on the dangerous world of the occult and the destructive consequences it has on peoples' lives. Also, on radio, on television, and in print, he addressed topics that were usually ignored, either because they were crushed by secular prejudices or because of the inattention of the Church. During his eulogy, Father Bamonte emphasized Amorth's "tenacious and passionate" attempts to reawaken the Church to the needs of persons who suffer in the spirit and therefore require the help of exorcists. It was Father Amorth, Father Bamonte recalled, who in 1991 gathered together all the Italian exorcists and then three years later founded the International Association of Exorcists, becoming its long-time president. The association's statutes were recognized on June 13, 2014. "Its only objective," Father Amorth emphasized, "was to obtain cures for the illnesses caused by demonic oppression." Never did he write a book, grant an interview, or appear in the media without having this objective in mind.

Father Antonio Mattatelli, of Lucca, one of the youngest Italian exorcists writes: "Whenever someone told him that he was the most famous exorcist, he would respond: 'The most famous but not the most effective.'" Father Amorth always referred to Father Matteo La Grua, another giant in the Catholic ministry of liberation, as the truest exorcist—and saint! But I believe that Father Amorth also was a saint, with his Modenese sincerity, always direct and never diplomatic. He was one who gave bread for bread. He was a master in every way: in chasing demons, in his ministry of the Word, and in his preaching and evangelization. He touched his listeners and his readers.

The great good he did as a Catholic priest for sixty-two years was centered on his devotion to Our Lady (including consecration to her Immaculate Heart), his exorcisms (it has been calculated that during his last thirty years, he did at least a hundred thousand exorcisms), and his books, which have influenced generations of believers.

If you will pardon the audacity of my affection and admiration (and ignore the decree of Pope Urban VIII that asked the faithful to leave judgment on the matter to the Church), I must say that Father Amorth was a giant, a teacher, an example of greatness, and therefore a saint. I was with Father Amorth one Tuesday morning when he was struggling with one of his patients in the Basilica of St. Paul Outside the Walls. He was sweating much from the heat, but also because of the fidgeting of the obsessions, so horrendous and at the same time fascinating. I witnessed this scene often; and each time, I was impressed with his familiarity with the procedure and with the throngs of people seeking him and asking him for help.

He received rivers of people in that "clinic of the spirit," always in control, secure, and charitable, when, as if overseeing an assembly line, he performed exorcisms in industrial quantities.

No one knew where he got that serene, psychic strength and how he found the time — with all the exorcisms — to churn out books. Yet all of us understood that it was Christ (along with His Immaculate Mother) who was the secret flame of the energy he poured into our beloved Church — the Church, as Benedict XVI said at Fatima, "where the faith is being extinguished in the heart of so many believers because it is not being nurtured."

I saw him for the last time on April 8 of last year, in Rome, at the Paulines' motherhouse. I was with some friends. I wished, above all, to ask him a question I could not answer about exorcisms, about the possibility that holy and saved souls could also manifest themselves, as devils do.

This field is difficult to understand and explain. But I wished to hear from him — the exorcist par excellence. And he answered me with his usual competence. "Yes," he said to me, "the saints at times manifest themselves: it has happened to me with St. Gabriele of Our Lady of Sorrows, St. Benedict, and St. Padre Pio of Pietrelcina, whom I knew during his life." Then he gave me a pat on the shoulder, adding: "Keep going, young man!"

Looking back, I am moved thinking of the beauty and greatness of that man, so lucid and wise but with an old, sick body that was going to ruin. I thought: "He is a saint! His heritage will be paradise!"

Father Antonio Rizzolo, director of the magazine *Credere*, remembers him, above all, as a person who has done much good for everyone: "I was struck by the gratitude expressed on the Internet by those thanking him for his ministry of exorcism, an undertaking he engaged in with dedication up until a few weeks ago, when his strength failed him. These simple, needy people found in him a compassionate listener. Here are a couple of testimonies: "Thank you, Father Amorth, for all that you have done for the people who needed you." "May the Lord receive you at His side." "Dear Father, protect us from above." "Thank you for all the good that you have done for us." "Now you are with the Lord."

I would like to remember Father Amorth as my confrere, a fellow Pauline. He was indeed part of my congregation, the Society of St. Paul. But I began to know him better in 1989, when I collaborated with him at the magazine *Madre di Dio*, which he directed during its first year and then continued as a contributor.

Father Gabriele was a gruff person only in appearance. Certainly, he was very frank, but he loved to joke. He was famous for his comic way of greeting you. In more recent times, I went to see him with another Pauline, Father Stefano Stimamiglio, to ask for advice about a new magazine, *Credere*, that I directed. He liked the idea of a publication that presented the Christian faith simply through life testimonies. He encouraged us and gave us his blessing. He also agreed to write a column on how to defend oneself from evil and grow in faith. The column, edited by Father Stimamiglio, was titled "Dialogues on the Hereafter"—although I had suggested "The Devil Is Afraid of Me"—and ran for more than a year. In the end, this is one of the messages that Father Amorth left us: "The devil is nothing against the mercy of God."

The American journalist Tracy Wilkinson, author of a book on the Vatican exorcists, described him in his element:

> Father Amorth receives his tormented flock in the building that hosts his office and accommodations and that of his confreres. His room is always distant from the street, so that no one can hear the screams. "Otherwise the police arrive," he says with a hint of a smile.
>
> The room measures about nine by fifteen feet; the walls are a sea green, broken off here and there by some cracks in the plaster. There are five or six straight-back chairs leaning against the walls and a lightly padded chair with a vinyl covering where patients who are not in very critical condition can accommodate themselves. The helpers are seated in other chairs; among these, there may be priests, family members and relatives of the patient, and assistants who help to control the patient. Amorth also turns to laymen, followers of the Catholic Charismatic Renewal, who often participate with their prayers. "Many prayers are needed," he says. Unstable or sick patients who might have to be tied down with straps are stretched out on a small bed with padding, similar to those used in medical offices. Amorth showed me the straps that are used for this purpose. Violence is always an eventuality; therefore, there are always assistants. Few priests practice exorcism alone.
>
> Amorth has hung eight crucifixes, some images of Our Lady, and a picture of St. Michael the Archangel on the walls. A statuette of Our Lady of Fatima sits on a small table in a corner. There are also images of Pope John Paul II, St. Padre Pio (Father Amorth's mentor); Father

Candido Amantini, and Father Giacomo Alberione, founder of the congregation of the Society of St. Paul. Amorth calls them his protectors, adding that the reintroduction of the image of St. John Paul II has proven to be particularly efficacious, because the demons become very irritable before him. At the top of the wall, there is a small window with an air conditioner and drawn curtains.

Father Amorth has the tools of the trade at hand: inside an old briefcase are two wooden crucifixes, an aspergillum for sprinkling holy water, and a vial of consecrated oil. In addition, he uses a purple priestly stole and a book of prayers with the official formulas for exorcism.

Father Francesco Bamonte, his successor in the International Association of Exorcists, offers this testimony:

> With the death of Father Gabriele Amorth, a great personality of the twentieth century has left the scene. It is significant that he died the same day as an eminent Italian statesman, Carlo Azeglio Ciampi (president of Italy 1999–2006).
>
> Gabriele Amorth was the youngest of five sons born to Mario and Giuseppina Amorth, in Modena on May 1, 1925. Gabriele felt the call to the priesthood from a very early age. Like his father, he studied law and was engaged in the Emilian social-political and ecclesial events of his time; he did much, in his young adulthood, to contribute to the common good. After the war, he joined Giulio Andreotti and other prominent Italian statesmen in the writing of Italy's constitution. When Andreotti joined the new government, Amorth chose the priesthood and religious life. Eventually this choice led him to the ministry

of exorcism; through his undoubtable communicative skills, he contributed greatly to this ministry's legitimacy with the people of God and the world at large.

The writer Angela Musolesi remembers him in this way:

Throughout the years he collaborated with various exorcists; for this I can affirm without fear of refutation that Father Amorth is the greatest exorcist. Not because he had more power to liberate, but for the totality of his work; he had more experience than all the others, since he practiced this ministry for more than twenty years and he learned it as an apprentice working with another great exorcist, Father Candido Amantini. During that period, he learned how to recognize the presence and action of the Evil One and how to liberate. This formation, learned at the side of an expert, is not a matter of minor importance. The one who follows a brief course for exorcists and is then officially nominated as an exorcist does not have full cognition of the facts, which it takes many years to gain (and several stories of vexed persons have confirmed it). Amorth also read a great deal on the topic and about related fields, deepening his knowledge and understanding of how the Satanists and occultists act. As a result, and as the global success of his books demonstrates, his teachings are the best. By following them, one can successfully liberate himself from the actions of the "fool"—Amorth's term for the devil.

Father Amorth is also the greatest exorcist because he is generous, as God is generous, and funny. During an exorcism, a demon accused him of being a glutton, and Father Amorth responded: "Well, what's it to you?"

If he had some doubt, he sent the person to a psychologist, but he often carried out the exorcism as a diagnostic tool, because, he argued, if a person has a need for an exorcism, fine; if not, the exorcism does no harm. He also carried out exorcisms over the telephone. In Italy, there are only two exorcists who have used this method: Father Amorth and one of his elderly friends—two priests for sixty million people. But why do so few avail themselves of this convenience? The effects are the same as for those who show up physically. Why limit God's mercy? In other countries, many exorcists interact with people by telephone. There are also other practical means of communication, such as Skype.

Father Gabriele Amorth was awarded a gold medal for military valor demonstrated during the war of the Resistance (1944–1945) against the fascist dictator. He earned another medal of valor for his resistance to the Evil One, for having fought in favor of the reign of Jesus. And he did it publicly.

Father Livio Fanzaga of Radio Maria shares his testimony: "Father Gabriele Amorth was a presenter on Radio Maria since 1990, and from our microphones he woke up the Church on the diminution of the ministry of exorcism. One of my first programs at Radio Maria, at that time a small parochial station, was a commentary on his book *An Exorcist Tells His Story*; it then became the title of his popular program at Radio Maria for twenty-five years."

Francesco, one of the many who went to Father Amorth for exorcisms, describes the priest's day:

Among the fixed collaborators, there was Father Stanislaw and at least three or four laymen who constituted a prayer group and assisted at restraining the patient. Each morning he began at 8:50 with the blessing of the water, salt and oil brought by a group of persons who evidently had a great need of it; in addition, there were always three or four persons who profited from it by asking for a quick blessing. The morning exorcism began at 9:00 with a half-hour pause between appointments for the paperwork. Each morning there were five appointments, mostly cases that were already known that came from Rome or somewhere in Lazio, although at times they came from adjacent regions, from the North of Italy and from abroad. In some rare cases, other prelates pleaded for appointments for their congregants, claiming the impossibility of finding a good exorcist in their dioceses.

The atmosphere of the little rectangular room where the exorcisms were performed was strange, nearly surreal; one gained access through a small door of wood and opaque glass. As soon as you entered, your glance was drawn to a worn-out armchair in brown velvet that served the less agitated patients. The ceiling was high, and the walls were white but a bit soiled in spots. Two windows provided illumination and warmed the room during the hot weather. But during the winter it was rather cold.

Under the window was a small bed with a faded green cover and a thick blanket at the foot where the patient would place his feet. Under the bed was a wooden box containing the tape and belts used to tie the more robust patients, generally men, to prevent them from doing harm during the prayer. I recall little of what happened during my attendance, but thinking back, I can now say that some people could not be held firm even with six or seven volunteers if they had not been tied; therefore, restraining them is a very useful precaution done for their own good.

On another wall is a bookshelf with diverse religious books, a Roman missal, some theological works, and a biography of saints. During the exorcisms, some folding chairs are brought into the room from the adjoining antechamber, which functions as a waiting room for the persons scheduled for exorcisms during the morning. The seats serve not only for Father Amorth and the relatives and friends of the persons exorcised, but also for the persons who assist, their relations, and the permanent helpers, Father Stanislaw, Christina, Rosa, and Teresa. In addition, there were now and then other laymen, brothers, seminarians, and priests from every part of the world who wished to participate in order to observe, learn, and especially help through their prayers.

Marco Tosatti Interviews Father Amorth

The Vaticanist Marco Tosatti has written much of Father Amorth and has coauthored books with him on his life and work. Tosatti describes Amorth as a smiling man with a playful air, who peppers his speech with jokes and who does not have a cell phone, does not know how to use the Internet, and does not watch television or read the newspapers. Amorth claims that, at dinner, his confreres inform him of world events and of the other unhappy things that acquaint him with his patients' world.

How are exorcisms understood from a historical perspective?

In the first four centuries of Christian history, all were able to do exorcisms; exorcists did not exist as we understand them today—that is, priests with a precise ministerial mandate. Jesus said: "In my name you will cast out demons." It was enough to believe in Him and to act with faith. And this remains true to this day.

Today we have groups of the Renewal and also individuals who do what I call "prayers of liberation." I do not call them exorcisms in order to distinguish them from true and proper exorcisms. But when prayers of liberation are done with faith, they are as effective as true and proper exorcisms. Eventually exorcism was founded as a minor order and entrusted solely to priests who were nominated by the bishops. Today it still functions like this; only bishops have the authority, the absolute monopoly, to name exorcists or to take back their right to do exorcisms.

When a priest prays a public prayer of liberation, which I call an exorcism, he is not carrying out initiatives performed by the exorcist in order to liberate a person from the devil; rather, he is praying a private prayer, the prayer given by Jesus, that all can pray.

Today many complain to me of the total absence of exorcists. And it involves first-rate nations: Germany, Austria, Switzerland, Spain, and Portugal, to mention just some of them. These countries do not have exorcists. Therefore, many faithful write to me, asking to come to Rome to receive exorcisms from me. And this is not possible, because I am overwhelmed with appointments and cases to follow. Therefore, I direct all of them to the Catholic Charismatic Renewal, or to those priests who do prayers of liberation, which, as I have already mentioned, if done with faith, have the same effect as a true and proper exorcism.

Father Gabriele, let us return to your personal experience. Before you were nominated by Cardinal Poletti, what did you think of the devil?

To be honest, it never occupied my thoughts very much. Yes I knew that there was a devil, and I believed in the Gospel. I am from Modena, but I never heard anyone there speak of the existence of exorcists. On the other hand, in those times, priests practically never spoke of the devil, possessions, or exorcisms. I was ordained in 1954, a Marian year, the centenary of the dogma of the Immaculate Conception. More than fifty years have passed, and the ministry of exorcism remains an extremely important subject that should be imparted to all who are preparing for the priesthood; even more so, because so many young people are no longer going to Church, but instead are getting involved with séances, going to wizards, fortune-tellers, and so on. Therefore, I think that it is very important to educate seminarians on these topics in order to keep people away from these dangers. And priests must be prepared to do the same. But a great many of the clergy know very little about these themes.

When, by chance, I happen to find myself before an evident case of diabolical possession, I understand that satanic actions and prayers of liberation do not belong solely to the past, when Jesus practiced His ministry, but they are also part of the present. Today Satan is trying more than ever to lead as many souls as possible to an eternal death.

From the beginning of my ministry, I understood that there are two opposing categories of possession: those who fall into error and sin and those who love God. I can confirm it by drawing it from Scripture and Tradition. I recall a case that touched me personally very much. An excellent seminarian left the seminary after two years and lost his vocation, because I did not exorcise him; it concerned a very delicate matter, on which I shall not go into detail. I can say, however, that for me it was a great revelatory shock, which made me understand how I had to act in order to oppose the action of the devil, above all when he tries to strike the consecrated: during the ten years that followed this incident, I saved many vocations by exorcising seminarians, priests, and religious.

Is the devil also in the Vatican?

Yes, there are many members of satanic sects also in the Vatican.

Who are they? Are they priests or simple laymen?

There are priests, monsignors, and also cardinals!

Excuse me, Father Gabriele, but how do you know?

I know it from persons who have referred them to me because they have a direct way of knowing it. And it is also often "confessed" by the same demon that is under obedience in the exorcisms.

Father Candido had the gift of discernment, an extraordinary discernment. He received patients only in the mornings and not on Sundays; yet he was able to receive about eighty persons a day and only in the mornings. He took them two at a time, pronounced a very brief prayer, and then he would say, "Return" or "Do not return." "Return" meant that there was something there, and "Do not return" meant that there was nothing demonic. He could also understand the situation just by looking in the face of a person. Furthermore, he was able to do a diagnosis solely from a photograph. It was necessary, however, for him to see the eyes clearly. At times, the eyes are covered or closed in a photograph. Oh, how many tumors he cured!

Unlike Father Candido, I have no particular charism of discernment, and in order to frame a single case, I need to do a diagnostic exorcism. I need the exorcism in order to see the reaction. Sometimes the exorcisms do not provoke any reaction. But then, when the patients go home, a day or two after, there is an improvement. And they telephone me to inform me of the improvement as if it is an extraordinary thing. Then they return, I do other exorcisms, and at that point, the improvement is immediate and the evil goes away.

But when they come the first time and I look at their reaction, it seems as if nothing has happened. Yes, it happens that they are moved and they cry out, but for certain persons, there is often no change following this reaction. Later on, they say: "You took that evil from me that no one could take away, but after you blessed me ..." I call them blessings in order not to frighten people with the word *exorcism*, and they are so efficacious that the evil goes away.

At times, after the first appointment, the effect has a limited duration. They say to me: "Father, after your blessing I was well for a month. Then the evil returned." I respond: "Let's repeat it. Perhaps you have need of a blessing once a month." So, each case is different.

In general, however, I can affirm that the head and the stomach are the two most vulnerable points. But the demon also strikes elsewhere: at times, he strikes the bones, at times the legs; many times he strikes the uterus or the genitals. And, after the blessing, they become normal again.

Father Gabriele, could you offer some clarifications regarding the various ways that one can cause an evil spell? In what way, that is, can the Evil One strike man?

To respond to this question, I refer to a descriptive chart on the evil spell that I have drawn from various authors and from personal reflections drawn from cases I have confronted directly. The evil spell is an evil procured through a demon. Depending on the objective, it has the following characteristics:

- amatory, in order to favor or destroy a romantic or love relationship with a person
- venomous, in order to procure an evil that is physical, psychic, economic, or familial [or a combination of these]
- binding, in order to create impediments to actions, movements, relationships
- transferable, to affect a person through torments done to a puppet or a photo of that person
- putrefying, to procure a mortal evil by subjecting a material object to decay
- possession: to introduce a diabolical presence in the victim

Depending on the manner, it can be defined as:

- direct: through the victim's contact with the object bearing the evil (for example, when one makes the victim drink or eat something cursed)
- indirect: through evil done on an object that represents the victim

According to the methods:

- through embedding and torture, with pins, nails, a hammer, sharp points, fire, or ice
- tying in knots or binding, with laces, knots, reins, ribbons, strips, or hoops
- through putrefaction, burying the object or the animal symbol after having altered it
- through malediction, directly on the person, or his photo, or on a symbol of the person

According to means:

- with the evil eye or a spell: piercing puppets or flesh with pins, bones of the dead
- with blood, toads, chickens

- with cursed objects: gifts, plants, cushions, dolls, charms, or talismans
- with a glance (evil eye), a touch of the hand, or an embrace
- by telephone: with silence then a breath, or in other ways

How many exorcisms do you do during the year? And how long does an exorcism last?

According to a rough estimation, I have done about sixty-thousand exorcisms. Not sixty-thousand persons, naturally. I cannot calculate the number of persons: I can calculate the number of appointments for exorcisms. Today I do about seventeen a day; before there were many more. For example, in the morning, which I reserve for the most difficult cases, I schedule five persons. Naturally, if someone does not have an appointment, there is nothing I can do, because otherwise I would go crazy.

At times, it happens that I may do hundreds of exorcisms for the same person; for this reason, I say I can calculate roughly how many exorcisms I have completed, but I cannot say how many persons I have assisted. I attempted to record the number of possessions I exorcised, but after I reached a hundred, I got tired, and I no longer kept track. Let us keep in mind that when I was named Father Candido's successor, I found myself with all those he left behind; I inherited all those in his care, among whom were those who were clearly possessed or tormented by the demon. I found myself with a crowd of people who were certainly disturbed by the demon. Thus, I began immediately with a clientele, among whom there were several who had a possession.

The exorcism should be done, if one has only one patient, every day; if not, at least once a week: therefore, more than fifty exorcisms for the interested party. But allow me to show you my calendar. At the top I write the morning appointments; below, those of the afternoon. Look here, the month of December, which is not even one of the busiest, is completely filled, including Christmas Day! As to the length of the exorcism, in general I do a half hour, but at times, it is not enough, because it is necessary to continue until the person revives. If one goes into a trance, it is necessary to wait until he becomes conscious. And let us note that when patients return to themselves, they are cheerful, content, and feel healed. But they are not healed. After a few hours or a day, they fall back into the same situation.

If you knew how many little notes I give them with the Ten Commandments! The first thing I look at is their medical history, documents, and analyses. Then I question them: I ask if they pray, if they go to Mass, if they go to Confession. I have a bunch of these papers, and I say: "Look at the Decalogue and study it well." I begin always with the Third Commandment: "Remember to keep holy the Lord's Day." Then I go to the Sixth, and I tell them: "Do not commit impure acts." This is not the most serious sin, but it is our weakness. The most serious sins are those of arrogance and pride. But the violation of the Sixth Commandment is also the most common sin; so that St. Alphonsus Liguori said: "One goes to hell precisely for this sin, and never without this sin." Everyone sins against this commandment. It is our greatest weakness.

One leaves the seminary and becomes a priest without ever having heard anyone speak of the devil or of exorcisms, or of the danger of wizards and the occult sciences, or of diabolical possession. And then, not believing in any of it, he never preaches it. I have had so many priests who come to assist at my exorcisms say: "Look, Father Amorth, before I came here, I did not believe; now I believe!" Jesus did exorcisms in the street. Now it is necessary to do them in secret.

Let us return to your experience. You are a member of a religious congregation. How do they regard your work?

As I said, an exorcist's ministry is difficult and misunderstood. I am also so loved that this is the twenty-third place where I have done exorcisms. In substance, the people do not wish to hear screams. I have been sent away from all the places where I did exorcisms here in Rome.

Is it difficult to live with the diffidence of your colleagues?

You get used to it.

Is it truly a battle on two fronts — on the part of those who should help you?

It is like this. The bishops, even those who nominate exorcists, in general do it unwillingly. They do not keep informed on how things are going, on how many exorcists there are, or on how many are needed; and they do not gather the exorcists together to examine the situation. They do none of this. They name someone, and then the exorcist is on his own, and that's it. They do not concern themselves.

What are the most common reactions among your "patients"? How do they demonstrate hostility toward the prayers of liberation during the exorcism?

There are very many who spit, and they try to guess the exact moment to get you. An exorcist with a little experience learns to defend himself from the spitting; so he tries to put a handkerchief or tissue in front of his face. Anyhow, I recall one who always spit, and I would see it coming in time, so I would put a hand in front of my mouth. Once, as he spit, three nails materialized in his mouth. I still have those nails. I keep them in my room on the third floor. Sometimes I bring these objects on television, because television needs props; so it is necessary to show things.

Is there a danger that an exorcist, like you, who struggles against the devil, who does exorcisms, who chases demons, may become arrogant?

Certainly! When I find myself doing exorcisms in the Church of the Immaculate Conception, and I may have ten persons helping me, I pontificate, my thoughts are on me, but during the exorcism I am focused constantly on the Holy Spirit: "Holy Spirit, intervene, I pray. You know that I am a good-for-nothing. You know that I am not worth anything. You intervene," I ask continuously, because one can give in to temptation even while preaching. I rarely go out to preach, only on very special occasions. And then I have people assailing me, trying to touch me; I am always surrounded by body guards for protection from people who wish to touch me. And I say: "Come on, why touch me? Smell me; I stink of salami!"

As a remedy for the sin of arrogance, I would like to recall the episode of a healthy kick.... During a prayer of liberation, knowing that the demon dislikes the sincere confession of sins, and repentance, we made a broad public confession of many sins. Then, each one approached the priest for a private confession and to receive absolution. As the last, I knelt before the other priest who was celebrating with me in order to ask pardon for all my sins, especially those that impeded me from performing my ministry well. At this point, I felt a good swift kick from one of the "patients" who had gotten away from the control of my collaborators. For me, that kick was healthy. Therefore, I extend its effects to all those who have need of a good push to confess their sins.

2

The Enemy of Father Amorth
by Marcello Stanzione

The Devil Goes by Many Names

The saintly Curé of Ars defined the demon as the "creeper"; an exorcist acquaintance from South Korea calls him the "louse" (*pediculus*); and Father Amorth called him the "fool." The Hebrew lexicon has no specific term that translates the term *devil* or *demon*, because it has been subjected to a long, complex evolution. The Greek translation (of the Seventy[1]) of the word *Satan* that is found in the Old Testament is *diabolos* and means adversary, or calumniator, deceiver (from *diaballein*). It occurs twenty-six times in the Old Testament and thirty-four times in the New Testament. Daimonion occurs sixty-three times (in

---

[1] The first translators of the Bible from Hebrew to Greek were called the Seventy. (Probably the number was rounded off for the conventional use of the abbreviation LXX. Actually, there were seventy-two.) According to the *Letter of Aristea*, at the request of King Ptolemy II Philadelphus (285–257 B.C.), seventy-two sages (scholars) came from Jerusalem to Alexandria, Egypt, to translate the Torah (Jewish Law) — that is, the five books of the Pentateuch — from the original Hebrew into Greek.

Matthew 8:31 in the form *daìmones*) and *diabolos* thirty-seven times.

Satan and *Diabolos* have been passed on to the various Christian languages; Satan, in particular, has remained unaltered from the original Hebrew; only the Italian language has added an *a*, transforming it into *Satana*; in Greek, Latin, French, Spanish, English, and German it has remained just as it is, *Satan*. *Diabolos* has remained more or less unchanged only in the Catholic languages of neo-Latin Romance origins: *diabolus* (Latin), *diavolo* (Italian), *diablo* (Spanish), *diable* (French); while in English it became *devil* and in German *teufel*. Before the word *teufel* was derived, there was a Gothic word *unhuplo* (which became *unhold* in German, meaning the "Evil One," a term also used in Italian for the devil) which was employed in place of the Greek *daimon*, and in the Gothic tradition of the Bible, it was adapted by Ulfilas.[2]

A peculiarity of the term *teufel* is that it is used as Satan and Diabolos in both the singular and the plural, *die teufel* (the devils); and because of the homophony, mitigates the difference between the "devil and the demons," which becomes "the devil and his angels," as the Savior emphasizes: "Then he will say to those at his left hand, 'Depart from me, you cursed, into the eternal fire prepared for the devil and his angels'" (Matt. 25:41). This citation occupies an important place in demonology, because it emphasizes the subordination of the bad angels to Satan—that is, to the devil.

The German demonologist Egon Von Petersdorff, a layman, thinks that it is advisable to substitute the plural, the devils, with

---

[2] Ulfilas: a Goth missionary from Eastern Germany of Cappadocian Greek descent credited with translating the Bible into the Gothic language; he participated in the Arian controversy.

the old expression, the demons, and thus to speak not of "the devil and his devils," but of "Satan and his demons." The Italian contains an idiomatic peculiarity, since, for the pagan spirits and the fallen angels of the Christian religious world, there are two words that are nearly synonymous; the first, "the demon," then plural "the demons." Such a distinction is very important, because, regarding the more elementary demonological questions, there is a chaotic confusion of concepts.

Pagans maintain that there are also good demons, which is contrary to Sacred Scripture and the teaching of the Church, which recognizes only bad demons. In the translation of the Old Testament, *devil* is found only in Wisdom 2:24. The literal sense in Greek, "calumniator," "sewer of discord," or "adversary," regards the rapport between God and man (1 Tim. 3:11; 2 Tim. 3:3; Titus 2:3). Therefore, the devil's activity presupposes the relationship of man to God that has already been established in creation.

The Old Testament's linguistic use of the term *Satan* merits particular attention. In it, one observes that the devil's biblical conception is not the fruit of a purely dualistic confrontation with God; rather, he originally is God's functionary or official. For example, in Zechariah 3:1, Satan is the accuser of Joshua, and in the prologue of the book of Job he is the "heavenly advocate" who, in a purely formal way, defends an interest of God. But he uses the power over man that comes to him from God in a way that already betrays his subtle intention. Particularly instructive, in this regard, is the passage in Chronicles (1 Chron. 21:1) where "Satan rose up against Israel" and "incited David" to take a census of the Israelites. Here one observes a theological correction of 2 Samuel 24:1, where it is God himself who incites David to such an operation. Now the author substitutes Yahweh with Satan and manifests a more advanced phase in the way of conceiving Satan. Stripping the image of God, which was originally more complex in the Old Testament religion, he gives it certain apparently contradictory traits. Only in the successive linguistic use of Judaism and in the New Testament do God and Satan clash in a way so unhealthy that the fall of Satan will be spoken of as wished by God (Luke 10:18; John 12:31; Rev. 12:9). Only then will the devil be understood as an anti-divine entity that possesses some type of personal features.

In the Old Testament, the history of men is characterized by sin even from the beginning, but the mythological figure of the serpent in the earthly paradise (the Garden of Eden) is identified with the devil only in the latter part of the Book of Wisdom, where it says that death entered the world because of the devil's envy (see Wisd. 2:24). Regarding the existence of Satan, Sacred Scripture offers a very wide range of texts. But they are not simple quotations cited in order to guarantee the doctrinal solidity of the dogmatic definition of Lateran Council IV: "The Devil and the other demons were created good by God ... but by themselves they made themselves bad." It is necessary to follow the same criterion that safeguards the seriousness of the Magisterium of the Church. Such a criterion consists in verifying that the inspired author, through whom the word of God is manifested, intends to affirm, with his own authority, in a precise context the existence of Satan.

Both the Old and the New Testament speak of the devil and demons, but the interest in the figure of Satan in biblical literature is concentrated in the Gospels. For this reason, in illustrating biblical demonology, theologians prefer to refer to the New Testament. In neither Testament, however, is there a precise description of the demons, their nature, or their aspect.

Instead, prominence is given to their way of being. Their names are merely designations that present their behavior and activity in a way that delineates an image. Thus, their actions in the world are emphasized over their appearance.

Under the heading "Devil," the theological encyclopedia *Sacramentum Mundi* affirms that the name *Satan* has a very broad meaning then converges into a single sense in the doctrine concerning the demons of late Judaism.

The writers of Sacred Scripture, especially the prophets, in order to avoid the risk of dualism and to safeguard the transcendence of God, speak very little of angels or demons. Therefore, the Old Testament reserves an extraordinarily limited place to this mysterious personage indicated with the term *demon* or *devil*. It does makes mention here and there, although rarely, of a figure with traits that resemble the devil's, but it does not speak of the personage. The powers that neighboring peoples attributed to demons, the Bible attributes to Yahweh: illnesses, calamities, and deaths. It is He, for example, who renders Miriam, the sister of Moses, leprous (Deut. 24:9); inflicts deserved punishment on violators of the law (Num. 11:1); sends painful serpents against the people (Num. 21:6); reserves the right to punish sins (Exod. 20:5–6); and leaves Israel to its enemies (Judg. 2:14; 3:8, etc.). Ignoring the distinction between wishing and permitting, the sacred author does not hesitate to represent God as a "tempter," not only in the way he "tempts" Abraham in order to prove his love (Gen. 22:1), but also in the way he hardens the Pharaoh (Exod. 4:21; Rom. 9:18) without denying his part, because it is also Pharaoh who "hardens his [own] heart" (e.g., Exod. 7:13–22).

In the same way, the spirit in the book of Samuel that "tormented" Saul, is not in any way represented as a demon; rather, it is "an evil spirit from the LORD."[3] An analogous evil spirit is also sent by Yahweh to incite the leaders of Shechem against Abimelech, the king of Israel.[4] Moreover, it is the "anger of Yahweh" that, in 2 Samuel 24:1, incites David to take a census of the tribes of Judah and Israel. David will recognize that he committed a gross sin in having taken a census and in having acted like a crazy person.[5]

In the first book of Chronicles (21:1), this temptation will no longer be attributed to Yahweh, nor to his anger, but to Satan (his name without the article), who plays the role of Yahweh's simple instrument, analogous to the angel he sent to destroy Sodom (Gen. 19:13); the "exterminators" charged with striking the firstborn of the Egyptians (Exod. 12:23); that which Wisdom will assimilate to the "omnipotent Word" that "in the silence of the night is launched in heaven bearing like a sharpened sword the irrevocable decree of God" (Wisd. 18:14–16); the angel of Yahweh who beats back 185,000 Assyrians (2 Kings 19:35; 2 Chron. 32:21); the "scourges of the Holy City" contemplated by Ezekiel (9:1); or the "angel of the Lord" that struck to death the two old calumniators of Susanna (Dan. 13:55, 59).

---

[3] "Now the Spirit of the LORD departed from Saul, and an evil spirit from the LORD tormented him. And Saul's servants said to him, 'Behold now, an evil spirit from God is tormenting you'" (1 Sam. 16:14–15).

[4] "And God sent an evil spirit between Abimelech and the men of Shechem; and the men of Shechem dealt treacherously with Abimelech" (Judg. 9:23).

[5] "But David's heart smote him after he had numbered the people. And David said to the LORD, 'I have sinned greatly in what I have done. But now, O LORD, I pray thee, take away the iniquity of thy servant; for I have done very foolishly'" (2 Sam. 24:10).

Under the name of "Adversary," Satan also appeared in the prologue in the book of Job (chapters 1 and 2). But it does not concern a demon; rather, it is one of the angels of the court of Yahweh who, like the other "sons of God," in the heavenly tribunal, seems to fulfill the function of public accuser charged with making justice and the rights of God respected on the earth. Thus, he acts in the interest of God and with His authorization.

The trials that rained down on Job come directly from God (1:11; 2:5); Satan is solely his instrument, and in the poem, Job speaks only of God (for example, 6:9; 7:19, 14:19–20; 16:12; 19:6–22). Moreover, behind Satan's apparent service to God, one perceives a hostile will, if not toward God, at least toward man; Satan targets not only Job's goods and flesh but also his soul and his justice, in which he does not believe. The accuser becomes nearly a tempter. Thus, the Old Testament seems to conform to the conception of the ancient East: that demons personify the powers of evil that can dominate man. In Babylonian literature, one finds a broad documented demonology, including magic rites, exorcisms, and liberation from demons. The ancient biblical world seems to have analogous concepts but with extreme reserve and nuances, when, for example, in rare texts, there is mention of the demons of the desert (see, e.g., Lev. 16:10; Isa. 13:21; 34:13–14).

It is necessary to wait until the end of the postexilic world to discover the distinction between the angelic and the diabolical world (see the book of Tobit). From this moment on, one sees the tendency to identify demons with the pagan divinities. It will only be in postbiblical Judaism that a true organic conception will be delineated: the demons are then described as fallen angels, accomplices of Satan, rebels against God, and enemies of man.

In the Gospels, at the beginning of Jesus' public life, the demons appear as tempters and corrupters of men (see Mark 1:13). The goal of the temptation is to pervert the dignity of Jesus, the Son of God, and to keep Him from the task of bringing the vital gift of the Word of God to men. The episode of the temptation seems to lay down dramatically the foundation upon which Christ builds His message in the sense that the Gospel is everything: Satan struggles with Christ to obstruct His mission. Indeed, he will even try to tear it away from Him or to set Him against His own disciples.... In this context, even the Resurrection of Jesus acquires a new meaning: it is the definitive victory over Satan, that is, over death, offered to man as a triumph of the salvific love of God.

The stripping of the powers [of the devil], having been verified on the Cross and in the Resurrection, will be definitively revealed in the Parousia (the second coming) of the glorious Christ. Meanwhile, the world and men are continuously exposed to the attacks of these powers, which are concentrated on the Church and her members.

The arms with which one can do battle are: faith and obedience; the works of justice and truth; vigilance; and the gift of the discernment of the spirits. But with which names are these forces identified? In the New Testament they are called principalities, powers, forces, or virtues, both singular and plural (Rom. 8:38; 1 Cor. 15:24; Eph. 1:21; 3:10; 6:12; Col. 1:16; see 2 Pet. 2:10; Jude 8).

The evil forces, both singular and plural, are also the princes: the princes of the world, the lords, the gods, the angels, the demons, the spirits, the impure or evil spirits, the spirits of evil, and the elements (e.g., Mark 3:22ff., John 12:31; 16:11; 14:30; 1 Cor. 2:6–8; Eph. 2:23).

Satan is also spoken of as the devil, and as Beelzebul and Belial. He is represented mythically as a serpent, a dragon, or a lion and he is called the Strong One, the Evil One, the Accuser, the Tempter, the Destroyer, the Opposer, the Enemy.

He also appears as the prince of this world, the prince of the power of the air, and the god of this aeon (eternity) (see, e.g., Matt. 9:34; 12:24; John 12:31).

The names are taken from the Old Testament only minimally. The name "demon" [in the version translated by the Seventy] comes, in the last analysis, from the Hellenistic sphere, whereas that of "powers" in the New Testament is taken from Judaism, especially from the apocalyptic circles, which borrowed from certain neighboring religions. Therefore, Jesus, the Apostles, and the early Christian community did not say anything about these powers, which were unknown in the pagan and Judaic culture that surrounded them. Apart from this, the New Testament does not show any interest in a theory or speculation related to such phenomena. Moreover, among the various appellations of the diabolical powers, there is a certain interchangeability.

The Synoptics, having learned from the evangelists how Jesus liberated the obsessed, by commanding the wicked spirit to leave the afflicted one, speak of demonic presences in a lively, realistic way. How effective were the synoptics in communicating the existence of the devil? Their way of describing demonic illnesses does not reflect the popular thought of that epoch; in the Synoptics, the demoniac is understood as a part of the redemptive mission of Jesus. In fact, according to the Synoptics, Jesus came into the world to build the Kingdom of God upon the destruction of the kingdom of Satan, which is not considered an abstract evil power, but a concrete reality that exists in the world. As a result, the wish to take away from the Synoptics the affirmation of the real existence of Satan would essentially transform such a message. Moreover, the affirmation of the existence of Satan on the part of the Synoptics, St. John, and St. Paul is the subject of broad, profound doctrinal writings of the Fathers of the Church and is the basis of the dogmatic definition of Lateran Council IV: "This is not an arbitrary teaching of the Church, but an essential truth tied to Revelation."

Once the Faith affirms that Satan truly exists, the phenomena that we refer to as the nefarious signs of his extraordinary action become a credible reflection of his reality as the Evil One. Paolo Sacchi seems to share this same affirmation when he states:

> The figure of the devil in his many disguises is not the fruit of fantasy.... The devil does not at all represent the triumph of aesthetics over logic; rather, it condenses upon itself the most rational demands of human thought before the problem of evil. The devil is that unknown that resolves a complex equation of I do not know what level, where one takes into account multiple factors not easily reconciled among themselves, such as the existence of a righteous God, of the liberty of man that makes himself such in the face of a choice between good and evil, in which one of the two terms that makes himself such in the face of a choice between good and evil, in which one of the two terms, the Light, is traced back to God, while the other, darkness, is impossible to bring back to us, at least directly.
>
> In the figure of the devil there is also the presentiment of evil as an organized force, since it has as a goal the destruction, not only of this one or that one, but of everything and everyone, and therefore it cannot be the

work of a simple evil spirit. The devil is a force that man feels both externally and internally. The devil of Judaism is not "that part of everything called darkness" by Goethe, nor is it death that goes to its place like the ancient Canaanite myth. The devil demonstrates that evil exists and always will, and is always out of place; because it is a force that opposes order and in no way can it be any part of a reassuring structure of being."

The powers have their place, and therefore their nature, "in the heavens," as the letter to the Ephesians indicates (1:21); they belong to the sphere of the "invisible" (Col. 1:16). They are a type of personal being—that is, "they are beings perceived by intelligence and by the will like interlocutors, ... rational and gifted with a will." They are also beings gifted with power (Eph. 1:21; Col. 1:16; Rom. 8:38). From the cited texts, one can establish the following:

- The names given to the powers reveal themselves and their own nature.
- The powers are not limited to having power; they exist as power.
- They possess this nature, taking possession of the world and of man, in order to show in these and through these (man and the world) their nature as powers (see Luke 13:11, 16; Matt. 12:22).
- Under the action of the powers, both the world and human existence appear in the perspective of death, because, in taking possession of them, they lead them to death.
- The passage in Genesis, without pronouncing his name, without instructing the reader about his nature, without

explaining his origin, just by unmasking his figure, informs us of what matters and guides our practical behavior. (It is the New Testament that will cultivate the seed of this passage for us.)

Going back to the beginning (Genesis): here, also, the author takes care to prevent the danger of dualism:[6] the serpent is a creature of God, "one of the animals of the fields that God has made" who will pay dearly for having opposed God (3:1; see 3:14). But the serpent is also a creature apart, gifted with a knowledge and ability that is superior to man's: he knows some things that Adam and Eve did not know, and, above all, he knows how to dominate man in order to triumph and ruin God's work. In the interest of advancing his plan, he concerned himself solely with the interests of man; his first words do not stir up any suspicion in the soul of Eve, who responded naïvely. But the dialogue, once initiated, already forecasts the outcome. The serpent takes heart: he does not believe in the seriousness of the prohibition or the threat: it's simply God's way of safeguarding His prerogatives; only the naïve would imagine that God would subject Himself to the interests of man. It is, to the contrary, in violating the prohibition that man would become like God, knowing good and evil. The serpent, sowing confusion, triumphs at the moment that man doubts the unconditional character of God's orders and the purity of His love.

But what can one mean by "evil"? Evil is not a thing; it is not a virtue; rather, it is structurally a privation. To say that evil does not exist is an unjust trivialization of evil, and evil is never trivial. One can say that evil is always a lack of perfection, a lack of conforming to one's nature; a misuse of liberty and the ultimate

---

[6] Dualism: the theory that there are two conflicting powers, good and evil, in the universe.

cause of evil is rooted in the use of liberty. Scripture also tells us that not all the evil that exists is done by man; indeed, originally, man committed evil, but he did it through a suggestion that came from a distance. If we read the story of Genesis attentively, we become aware that it does not authorize an abandonment of responsibility; it does not say that since Adam and Eve were tempted (tricked) by the devil, they were not responsible. It says only that the temptation was very strong and that there is still an evil presence that in some way precedes man's every action. Evil, we could say, has a metaphorical dimension that is precisely this presence of evil spirits that have become such through a perversion of their will. This is alluded to in Scripture regarding the creation of the angels, and then their fall. In Scripture, we do not have such open affirmations, or at least none so important as those of the creation of the world and man, but we find some allusions that are sufficiently clear.

In the Second Letter of St. Peter (2:4) and in the Letter of St. Jude (6), we find some rather explicit passages that regard the Fall, while St. Paul, speaking of the principalities and powers, says that they are creatures (Rom. 8:38). To deny the existence of demons or evil spirits is to fall into Manichaeism, which the Gospel refutes. We find this fatal denouement, for example, in those Protestant theologians who affirm that the demons are "mental structures." What does this mean? That evil has its objective consistency, or that the demon is an evil inclination in the heart of man. It is a very ancient theory that we also find in the Talmud. But the problem has been shifted: if, in the heart of man, there is, even from birth, an evil inclination, then this inclination comes from God.

Many of these theologians affirm that Jesus, like all men of His time, shared the same concept of the existence of demons, angels, et cetera. This is inaccurate, because, even in Jesus' time, there were groups that denied the existence of devils and angels; the Sadducees, for example, denied the existence of angels (see Acts 23:8). Moreover, it is clear from the Gospels that the Lord often openly contradicts the convictions that are widespread in His times, demonstrating His complete independence.

The cannier research has verified that the book of Revelation, more than a "literary genre," constitutes a theological thesis. Therefore, the fundamental approach to Revelation should concern not its method but its content. Now, the core of its apocalyptical content is the problem of evil, where the demon no longer represents a symbolic figure, but is the substance of the solution: evil is not "something"; it is the mistaken use of liberty; thus, it has a personal foundation. The struggle against evil is then dramatized, and it has for an objective not the irrepressible laws of nature, but personal powers that can be conquered and forces of evil that can be weakened. Here we have the paradox and ambiguity of the apocalyptic message with all its dramatic power and dazzling hope.

The doctrine of faith of Lateran Council IV declares: "God, one and triune, is the creator of all things, visible and invisible, spiritual and corporeal, that with his own omnipotent power at once from the beginning of time created from nothing each creature, namely the angelic and the mundane and then man, constituted, as it were, of both spirit and body."

Therefore, Satan, like all creatures visible and invisible, was created not from all eternity but at the beginning of time. Satan, therefore, is a creature of God and a person. But there is a difference between the personality of man and that of Satan: man is a person composed of soul and body, whereas Satan is an angel that in perfection is greater than man because he is a "pure spirit," and therefore totally independent of matter. It is appropriate to specify, however, that this doctrine of the pure spirit of the angels and of Satan has no comparison in Scripture and in nearly all the Tradition of the Church Fathers, who point to a subtle, spiritual corporeity.

Although no council has ever defined the pure spirituality of the angels, the Church has accepted the doctrinal refinement on angelology of the High Scholasticism, above all, that of St. Thomas Aquinas. Today, in fact, theologians accept both the certainty of the doctrine, although undefined, and the affirmation of the pure angelic spirituality; and even though it is inadvisable, it is not heretical to reject it. The visible apparitions of angels or of Satan do not contradict this theory, even when they make use of material elements in order to make themselves present to a person or in a place, and it is always with the consent of God.

Before Father Amorth became a feisty exorcist, even with the typical frankness that characterized him, he was a sweet, affable, accepting man. Moreover, he had an innate empathy toward those who went to him seeking help. With a nearly teasing tone, he was capable of playing down each situation, even the most distressing. Many saw in him the figure of Christ the Healer, who turns toward the suffering and the demoniacs in order to liberate them from their evils and from the devil. The long line of persons who walked past his casket, rendering him homage before the funeral rites, testifies to all the good he had done.

Father Amorth Speaks of the Devil

In one of his last books, Father Amorth says of the devil:
In my life I had to respond to an infinite number of questions on exorcisms. The first, that always came back, was: "Are there

exorcists who are stronger and more capable than others?" I do not deny that there are differences between one exorcist and another. But what the differences are is always difficult to evaluate. There are spiritual factors—for example, the intensity of prayer, the union with God and sacrifices; and then there are human factors, such as experience, intelligence, culture, and intuition. But often everything is relative. Some exorcists function better with certain demons and not so well with others. But I repeat, the motive is difficult to explain. A French exorcist, responding to his bishop, who had asked him this question, gave him a list of new things he had learned year after year during the practice of this ministry. In substance he wished to say: "I can only make comparisons with myself, and I have noted that I always have something to learn, but I have also seen the advantage of having experience." Of course, in order to arrive at liberation from the demon, various factors come into play: the depth of the faith and prayer life of the person struck by the demon and those close to him; faith in the intercession of the Church; and lastly, the engagement of the exorcist as an instrument of God, through the Church. I also note that certain exorcists are more efficacious with a certain type of evil spell; others with another type. But then it is always the Lord who decides and who grants the grace of the results to whom and as He wishes. One owes thanks to Him alone.

Another question frequently asked of exorcists is the difference between a wizard and an exorcist. It is important to know the response, because often people go to those whom they should absolutely never go. The wizard, when he is a true wizard and not a swindler, acts with the power of Satan, whereas the exorcist acts with the power of Jesus' name and the intercession of the Church. And this is something that all must know.

The wizards, if they are truly such, are disciples of Satan, and therefore they can do nothing other than bring the accosted person down lower, even to desperation, nothingness, and endless suffering. There are no benefits to seeing a wizard, in any way and for any reason. If, by chance, initially one feels better, one immediately loses that small benefit and plunges deeper than before.

I have known so many persons whose lives were completely ruined because they went to a wizard. In any case, it is necessary to remember that, besides the help of exorcists, prayers are efficacious, if they are done with faith, humility, and charity (therefore without any material interest).

Praying for one another is a recommendation that comes to us from God. Each one can do it in conformity with the faith that he derives from his baptism—that is, the priesthood of his baptism; and it is even more efficacious with the ministerial priesthood. These are cases of private prayer that have nothing to do with the sacramental of exorcism. But they are prayers that bear much fruit.

I know so many who pray or bless effectively; but then, I also know those who have made themselves famous as wizards, even when they are nothing more than tricksters or hypocrites, not even true wizards. We cannot pretend that it is ecclesiastical authority making pronouncements in these cases; there are too many, and they do not deserve official recognition. We must have good sense and know how to rule ourselves, and pastors must be able to give the appropriate advice in individual cases that present themselves in their parishes. And they must say to everyone: do not turn to wizards for any reason.

Let us say a little more about wizards. And let us ask ourselves again: Is it a sin to turn to wizards? Yes: Resorting to a wizard is a sin of superstition, a sin against the First Commandment and something that is expressly condemned by the Bible.

It can happen that one goes to a wizard and receives some benefits. But experience teaches that more often, these are temporary healings, which then dissipate, and greater evils take over. In each case, the unfortunate person is cured by a wizard who is connected to Satan. As a result, through the wizard, he is making a contract with both, and these ties come with difficult consequences, which are then very tough to break.

There are also fortune-tellers. To go to fortune-tellers is a sin of superstition, which can be serious. For example, one goes to hear what the cards say of him, out of pure curiosity. It is a venality that exposes a person to the risk of becoming involved, of entrapment.

Fortune-tellers are usually divided into three categories: first, the swindlers who make money off the naïve; second, those who have some paranormal power and use the cards to make use of it, as a diviner makes use of a dowsing rod to find water; and lastly, there are the fortune-tellers who practice with magic cards joined to divination.

Exorcists are another matter. They are effective because in exorcisms it is Christ who works. They can also do exorcisms at a distance. I often exorcize effectively by telephone.

What cannot be done is an exorcism against the will of a person. The Lord offers His gifts; He never imposes them. For example, I often heard from people recommended by members of their families who considered them demoniac. But these people did not pray; they did not ever go into a church; they did not believe; and they would never accept being blessed by a priest. In these cases, one can only pray.

There are two other questions that are often asked. The first: Can an exorcist err? For example, one hears: "I brought my relative to an exorcist, and he did not find anything." Or: "But his behavior is such that it makes one suppose there is an evil presence, and a sensitive affirmed that he is a victim of an evil spell. Is it possible for an exorcist to err?" In cases like this, I would advise listening to the opinion of another exorcist. Let us not forget, however, that there are some troubled persons who go from one exorcist to another until they find someone who tells them what they wish to hear. In this case, a good medical doctor is needed; or a series of prayers of liberation for specific fixations, if the subject is willing to cooperate.

The second question: What are the principal obstacles that the exorcist encounters? There are obstacles in doing a diagnosis, even with the help of medical specialists. And if one does verify an evil of diabolical origin, many obstacles may result from the patient's lack of cooperation. For example, the person may object to having a sincere conversion to God, living a life of grace, praying much, and receiving the sacraments frequently.

People are lazy; often they have a tendency toward passivity; I'm asked: "Father, liberate me from the demon." "No," I often respond, "you must liberate yourself. I can only help you and show you the means."

Sometimes there are impediments to grace: the difficulty of a sincere, heartfelt pardon; the difficulty of changing a lifestyle that is rooted in sin; the difficulty of breaking certain ties with the Evil One that require breaking off certain human ties: sinful friendships, rooted vices. The task of the exorcist is to bring souls to Christ: it is Christ who liberates. Everything that obstructs a life of union with God is an obstacle for the work of exorcists.

THE DEVIL IS AFRAID OF ME

Padre Pio and Fr. Amorth

It is important to emphasize the spiritual rapport between Father Amorth and St. Pio of Pietrelcina, which Father Amorth often recalled. He says:

I was a follower of Padre Pio for twenty-six years. I went the first time in 1942, during the war, and I was faithful to him until 1968. I remember two Masses: the first Mass, which made such an impression—then all the intermediary Masses—and the last Mass, at which I assisted. It lasted an hour and forty or fifty minutes.

At the first Mass, while he was at the altar, one could see that he was trying to mask his sufferings in every way. Those who were acquainted with his ways showed me how he would pretend to be using his handkerchief to dry the perspiration, but he was drying his tears, because he cried and suffered so much during the Mass. I saw at times when he knelt during the genuflections of the Mass and did not seem to have the strength to raise himself up. I remember all this together with the sufferings that he tried to mask, and I found the explanation for it in his famous response to Cleonice,[7] when she asked him how he felt when he was at the altar: "I feel like Christ on the Cross." Truly he lived the Passion. We always say, and it is theologically exact, that the Mass is the renewal of the Passion of Christ; it is bloody. And I would say, from the point of view of a celebrant, that Padre Pio, each time he celebrated Mass, was a bloody celebrant. Padre Pio suffered immensely; he relived the Passion.

---

[7] Cleonice Morcaldi was one of Padre Pio's spiritual daughters. She wrote a book about it: *La mia vita vicino a Padre Pio* (My life near Padre Pio).

44

As a young priest, I knew nothing of exorcisms. The first contact I had with this type of phenomenon was at Torbole Casaglia, in the Po Valley, near Brescia. There was a pastor there, Father Faustino Negrini, who was celebrating forty years as a priest, and he asked me to come and preach during the series of Masses and celebrations. (I preached five times that day.) Father Negrini had been rector of the Marian Sanctuary of Stella at Concesio, where Paul VI was born; and then he became an exorcist. During a chat, he spoke to me of an exorcism that he was doing, and he took me to visit this person.

Her name was Agnese Salomoni. She was a girl of fourteen, his parishioner, who was struck by a demonic possession. When he asked the devil: "Why have you taken this girl?" he responded: "Because she is the best of the parish." The bishop gave him the authority to exorcise her, although he was not yet an exorcist. At times, the bishop gives the authority to exorcise a particular person, and only that person. So, for thirteen years, he exorcised her. He also brought me to visit her at the hospital (Ospedaletti Bresciano). She was liberated at the age of twenty-six, and during that long period, he took her once to Padre Pio. He made the trip by car from Torbole Casaglia to San Giovanni Rotondo. It was a terrible journey because the car would stop all the time. The driver would look under the hood, and everything was fine, there was no problem. Then Father Faustino would pray and do exorcisms, and the car would function again, and the demon would laugh. It was a disastrous trip. After they arrived at San Giovanni Rotondo, the demon became terrified of Padre Pio. But while there, when Father Faustino presented the girl, Padre Pio gave her a blessing, and nothing happened. And then, during the return, the demon was triumphant, and there were no obstacles, and the demon made the victory sign at Padre Pio, as if to say,

"I won." As one can see, even Padre Pio did not always liberate people. The Lord has His plans. But I believe that Padre Pio also had a particular perception; he knew, he discerned whether a demoniac was mature enough to be liberated. He understood that that was the situation. He even gave a blessing, and the girl remained exactly as she was. Nothing happened.

I remember another young woman, a demoniac, who went to San Giovanni Rotondo. Her presence caused a sensation—there were cries and screams and all the rest—but she was not liberated by Padre Pio. It was not yet time, evidently. God has His plans for people. The liberation, the moment of the liberation, depends on many factors—how the possession began, for example. There are persons who have done everything: they have practiced magic, or even witchcraft; persons who have entered satanic sects, or have done some evil toward others with cursed instruments and remain possessed. Then they convert, but liberating these persons takes many years. I am content if, in a mildly serious case, a person is liberated within four to five years of exorcisms. I have had rare cases of liberations in a few months. I had a case, I would say, that was liberated in one and a half months, but I am not certain.

I would say that Padre Pio had a particular discernment for understanding whether a person was ready for liberation or not. Once, a priest accompanied a young man, supported by two robust friends, who, at Communion, would usually shout and forcibly dislodge himself from their grip. At the sight of Padre Pio, the young man began to tremble. Padre Pio fixed his gaze on him and said one phrase: "Go away from him." At that moment the young man was liberated. But liberations of that type are extremely rare.

3

A World Adrift
by Marcello Stanzione

Many Modern Trends Threaten the Faith

All the world appears enormously transformed with respect to the past, even the recent past: changes in the sociocultural, political, economic, and above all, religious order are continually happening. In a society dominated by fragmentation and a crisis of values, Catholicism has also come under attack and risks being degraded and marginalized and thus becoming an insignificant minority in a culture dominated by social customs that are growing ever more inhuman. In reference to the adolescent crisis of identity and the search for security, one notices an approach to new forms of religiosity—the New Age, sects, occultism, and the Eastern religions—as an alternative to the Catholic Faith, which is increasingly regarded as an archaic religious creed and next to collapse.

Young people today have many positive traits, such as generosity and social sensibility; but there is also a "youthful uneasiness," an identity crisis that is manifested by confused thinking that is the fruit of ideologies and of change and complexity. As a result, there is insecurity and a fragmentation that is often demonstrated by a lack of verifiable values, such as great ideals and ambitious projects. Therefore, in this context, which is a *crisis of values*, young people take refuge in the *cult of the individual* (exacerbated even to individualism), in the desire for *instant gratification* (hedonism), consumerism, the cult of the body and leisure, and the search for security through friendship and gratifying relationships.

Among the young, there is a prevailing mistrust of institutions and a fear of engagement; and these negative sentiments inspire an attachment to the transitory. Meanwhile, the distancing from the Catholic religion follows its course: although the attraction to atheism is limited, disinterest and indifference [toward the Faith] is increasing, and with it is a diminishing interest in religious practices, confession, and prayer.

Today young people are experiencing a crisis of the family. The patriarchal family of peasant origin no longer exists; it has been substituted by the nuclear family (parents and one child), the family that Rapoport[8] defines as "a double career," where the parents are distracted by reaching their career goals at any cost.

The nuclear family is not the only existing model for today's family; there is also the family formed by parents not legally married; the single-parent or broken family that is composed of only one parent and children; and the "multiple" family or extended family that may comprise a married couple, children born from their marriage, and those born from other previous relationships. To this group one can add the ex-spouses and their current partners.

Parents who are grappling with their careers may tend to neglect their children and their need for dialogue and listening,

---

[8] Rhona V. Rapoport (1927–2011), sociologist, author of *Dual-Career Families* (London: Pelican Books, 1971) and many other titles.

because the demands of their professional lives leave less space for the adequate care of personal relationships; as a result, many children and adolescents tend to resent it.

Some parents try to compensate for this lack of communication with their children by offering them material goods—beautiful clothes and generous allowances—but they do not spend time playing with them, speaking to them, and tuning in emotionally to their deepest needs.

There is, then, a great crisis of the family that involves a notable decline in values and of solid and valid points of reference for raising young people. Today so many of the boys and girls who are charged with bullying are solely waiting for someone to love them, understand them, and listen to them.

One of the effective ways to win the battle against emptiness and nihilism is the new evangelization. Evangelization is a turning point and a challenge, but above all, it is a mission that brings salvation to so many young people who risk falling into the trap of sects and of Satanism because their spirituality is being influenced by the cultural climate of egocentrism, narcissism, individualism, and materialistic values.

Two important cases that permit us to continue to hope are those of the seventeen-year-old American Cassie Bernall and that of the Italian Michaela. Cassie was led astray through the consumption of alcohol and experimented with self-inflicted wounding. She became obsessed with vampires and death, and she loved the satanic music of Marilyn Manson. She even thought of killing her parents. But, at a certain point, her life changed, and this tells us that nothing and no one is irredeemable. Cassie began to attend a Christian youth group, and Jesus held a place in her heart; from then on, she bore witness to her conversion and faith everywhere, until the day of her dramatic death on April

20, 1999. Two boys entered her school, Columbine High School, in Littleton, Colorado, and killed thirteen people, students and teachers. Before killing them, the young assassins asked each one, including Cassie, if they believed in God. Cassie responded yes, and so they killed her and the others who gave the same response. Through her yes, Cassie wished to demonstrate the courage that inspired her faith.

Michaela is the pseudonym of a person who took the name in homage to St. Michael the Archangel. This girl joined a satanic sect in Italy. When the sect planned to kill the foundress of the Christian association New Horizons, Michaela understood that she could not remain in it. With all the strength of her willpower, she decided to abandon Satanism, and she was accepted into the New Horizons group, where, after an intensive period of psychological-spiritual training and exorcisms, she was finally liberated from the evil that possessed her during her participation in the black masses. Unfortunately, many of today's young are fatally attracted to sects and new religious movements, and as a result, they distance themselves from the content of their Faith and the practice of living the Christian life. Therefore, it is necessary to promote a new evangelization in favor of Christian youth who live in these risky conditions.

The evangelical task of the Church is carried out concretely through a catechumenal action, which includes the whole set of activities directed at those who care about the Faith and want to become or become again Christian. It is the ecclesial presence and action in the world that promotes the transformation of society through evangelical testimony and educational and cultural action and by promoting peace.

Countering the evangelical task is the disturbing popularity of the Harry Potter stories, which have sold more than 350 million copies and have been translated into sixty-five languages. Father Amorth, as the most noted Pauline exorcist, has clearly affirmed that the Harry Potter books could have a bad influence on some children, pushing them toward a morbid interest in the occult. If we truly wish to help children and young people turn away from books poisoned by occultism it is necessary that parents and teachers have them read good books containing beautiful stories that are entertaining and educational, where the presence of magic (we think of the traditional fables) is solely an instrument for the moral of the story and not the substance on which the story is centered (as in the case of Harry Potter). They must also make space for Sacred Scripture and the biographies of the saints, which show us the marvelous face of God: they are infinitely more true, beautiful, and fascinating than the witchcraft and wonders that the demons perform in order to lead man to eternal damnation.

One may ask why there is so much need for exorcists. Why does it seem that the devil is enjoying and tormenting so many persons?

Satan has had a large group of followers since God first created man. Therefore, man has always had to struggle against the temptations and possessions of the demons, who act out of hatred of God. But today there is a denial of God that is to be feared. Today man has been able to impose a culture in which reason and science are enough to explain everything. God, from whom everything comes, is denied. And the result is mathematical: whoever denounces God gives himself over to the devil and to all his works. The Lord has spoken clearly: either you are with Christ, or you are with Satan. There are no alternatives or half measures. Today, as never before, there are many who either believe in Satan or who believe that he does not exist. Thus, he can operate in total liberty, tempting and tormenting men in a thousand ways, without having them think that these evils come from him.

Father Amorth Criticizes
Denial of the Devil's Reality

The following are some of Father Amorth's responses to questions from the writer Angel Musolesi [that address the reality of the devil].

They say that one should not speak so much of the devil. Is the devil spoken of too much?

Pope Francis spoke of the devil in his first ten discourses, and he speaks of him often. Furthermore, he has consecrated the Vatican to St. Michael the Archangel, in order to defend it from the Evil One. But, apart from this, the devil is not spoken of too much; it is necessary to do so more. All priests should speak of him continually.

So many, even in the Church, do not believe in the action of the devil? Why is this?

This is so. They do not believe in the existence of the devil or in his actions. But I insist on an extremely strong phrase spoken by Jesus Christ: "Who is not with me is against me" (see Matt. 12:30). Since Satan is against Him, it is as if He is saying: "Who is not with me is with Satan." There are no half measures. Either one is with Jesus, or one is with Satan. Even if one believes a little in the devil and does not believe in the words of Jesus, one is with the devil. Scripture, especially the Gospels, and the Fathers of the Church speak repeatedly of the devil and of his action in the world.

Certain priests preach that when the Gospels speak of Jesus'
liberating from the devil, it is only symbolism, not real.

It is not so. They are distorting the Gospel.

Why do so many pastors, in their homilies, belittle the action
of the devil, and why do they refuse to help persons and say to
those who are troubled: "It is nothing. Just say a prayer and
everything will go away"?

They are wrong. The devil is extremely powerful. The pastors
must be told to reread Sacred Scripture. St. John says: "The whole
world is in the power of the Evil One" (1 John 5:19). What more
does one need? Twice Jesus calls him "the prince of this world"
and St. Paul calls him the "god of this world" (see John 12:31;
14:30; 2 Cor. 4:4).

Why does the devil still rage in the world, since the world
has been consecrated to Our Lady, who has asked the people
to fulfill the practice of the first Saturdays of five consecutive
months?

The world is under the action of the devil because the world is
far from God: the people do not confess their sins, they do not go
to church, and they do not believe. Few put into practice these
devotional acts; they are a minority. This explains why the devil
tramples man in the world.

Let us speak of the prayers of liberation, because there is
much confusion regarding them, even among priests. There
are fairly well-known exorcists who write and affirm that
the substantial difference between exorcism and the prayers
of liberation is that the exorcism has a direct command and
the prayers of liberation can only implore God to act; they

do not have a direct command to the devil. Is it true? Is this the difference?

No, it is not true. We must always begin from the Gospel, because the instruction comes to us from there. "Those who believe in me [therefore, men and women, adults and children] will, in my name, cast out demons, [and] cure the ill" (see Mark 16:17–18). It is necessary only to have faith in Jesus and faith in the power of the name of Jesus.

Various exorcists maintain that certain prayers of liberation cannot have the direct command. For decades on Radio Maria, you have said, and you also write, that the prayers of liberation are private prayers and therefore can be both imploring and imperative toward the devil. Why, in your view, do they continue to say that a mother cannot say a direct command to the devil for herself, for her own problems, or for her child or her husband?

They are mistaken; they can very well command the devil. Persons can ask God, as in the Lord's Prayer, or they can command the devil to go away, above all for themselves and for their family members. "In the name of Jesus, Satan, go away!" Anyone can say it.

To whom do you advise it?

I advise it to anyone who has some vexations. Priests, nuns, and charismatic groups can do prayers of liberation for anyone who has need of them, and they chase the demons with optimal results. The prayers of liberation have the same goal and the same efficacy as the exorcism, with the difference that they can be recited by anyone, and I repeat, in particular, by priests and by nuns. I rely very much on laypeople and on prayer groups.

These persons, in the name of Christ, order the Evil One to abandon the body of the possessed; they invoke the help of the saints, the intercession of Our Lady, and, gripping a crucifix, they recite the prayers of command to the Evil One. They need only avoid the phrase: "I exorcise you." Rather, they [must] say continually: "In the name of Christ, go away, I cast you out, unclean spirit!" I know numerous cases of possessions liberated by non-exorcist priests or by laymen, because of exorcists who, wrongly, act without believing in the devil and without trusting in God.

Is there need of authorization from the bishop to pray prayers of liberation?

No, there is no need, because they are private prayers directly authorized by Jesus.

Can they be done anywhere, in any place, and at any moment? I ask this because often one has difficulty finding a place to do it.

If one has difficulty finding a place in a parish, one can go to a theater, a cinema, or a room in a restaurant. I have preached and held conferences in restaurants: if there is a large room, one can do it. And prayers of liberation can also be done in this way.

You often say and have written that prayers of liberation can be even more efficacious than an exorcism and that St. Catherine of Siena, who was not a priest or an exorcist, liberated those whom the exorcists did not liberate. On what does the effect of the prayer depend?

It depends on faith, on faith in Jesus and in the Gospels.

Several persons complain of being victims of curses and of not being able to liberate themselves from the effects of the spell that these produce in their lives. Can there be curses, then, that are not concretized in possessions?

A curse always becomes a vexation, and exorcisms are done even if there is only a vexation, which is an evil influence. The *Catechism of the Catholic Church* is clear: an exorcism is done even when there is no possession.

But some exorcists, if they do not see that there is possession, do nothing.

They are mistaken. If there is a vexation, that is, an evil influence, the *Catechism* says that an exorcism should be done.

Can the demons manifest themselves in dreams?

Rarely, but it is possible. One recognizes it from the fear that it causes the person. But if one invokes the name of Jesus or Mary, it goes away.

Does a curse cease with the death of a person?

At times, yes; at times, no; but more often no. I had a case of a mother who cursed her son and then repented. She asked her son to forgive her. She asked God to pardon her, and on her knees, she asked God to remove the curse, but there was nothing that could be done. The curse ceased only with exorcisms.

Curses are extremely powerful. And there are so many who go around cursing this one and that one! Above all, the curses of blood, of relatives and family members, are terrible. But blessings are also extremely powerful. It would be necessary that all who are involved be blessed, above all, mothers and their children.

"I regret the evil I have done; I wish to put it right." What can we advise a person who says this? What must the person do?

Acts of reparation.

And when someone has been subjected to a spell, other than following a correct sacramental life and getting exorcisms or prayers of liberation, what else can he do?

Heartfelt forgiveness toward the one who did this evil is the basic requirement. If there is no heartfelt forgiveness and one is subjected to exorcisms, God does not liberate. At times, I am made to understand that the exorcisms on a particular person are not having any effect, and I ask this person: "Have you forgiven the one who did this evil to you?" "No." And then enough with the exorcisms. One must at least make an effort to pardon the one who has done evil to us.

Forgiveness also occurs through the action of the Holy Spirit — that is, through the love of God, who alone can cure hearts. Therefore, one should invoke the Holy Spirit.

Some priests say that they cannot recite the exorcism of Leo XIII because it is not included in the current Ritual for exorcists. The exorcism of Leo XIII was present only in the old Ritual for exorcists, which was in Latin; and it has not been cited in the new Ritual, which is also in Latin and which has not been translated into the vernacular. Is that correct?

The exorcism of Leo XIII has not been translated, and it was present only in the old Ritual for exorcists. But people can say it.

Cardinal Suenens, one of the founders of the Catholic Charismatic Renewal, in his book Renewal and the Powers of Darkness, *asked for a reevaluation of the "prayer of liberation," which he hoped would also bring new vigor to the ordinary pastoral care. He maintained that it would help to support the charism of healing, especially interior healing. Do you agree?*

From my experience, it is fundamental. On the other hand, Jesus cured the soul first, then the body.

In your opinion, are the healing therapies of the charismatic groups useful?

Yes.

You often speak of the importance of consecrating oneself to Our Lady, the Virgin Mary. Do you renew your consecration in your daily prayers?

Yes, I do it daily. It is not an obligation; the important thing is to put one's life and all one's actions under the protective mantle of the Virgin Mary, entrusting oneself to her, trusting in what the Lord sends us. She said: "Let it be done unto me according to your word."

At Fatima, during the apparition to the children, there was the vision of the demons and the damned who were crying out among the flames. There was desperation, as you know. The Virgin Mary also asked for the consecration of Russia and for Communion on the first Saturday of five consecutive months. For those who do it, the consecration has been done, but—

Wait a moment. Above all, it is necessary to clarify that, at Fatima, what was more impressive was the vision of the damned souls.

Concerning the consecration of Russia ... I have my doubts that the consecration of Russia ever occurred in the way Our Lady requested it, because Russia was not named. Therefore, I believe that the consecration of Russia has not yet occurred.

There are priests who say to normal persons that it is not a good idea to recite the Rosary with someone who has some vexation even if he has no possession. What do you think of this?

They can recite the Rosary with these persons, as I do. Indeed, they should do it. It can be done for the good of all. The holy Rosary should always be recited; it is not ever unadvisable.

One often sees you in the mass media, especially in television transmissions. You are the only exorcist who exposes himself so much. Have you been criticized for being a public persona and always saying what you think?

I go on television often and wherever they invite me. I always say to whoever questions my way of doing things that I wish to bring Jesus everywhere, even to the doors of hell. Only in this way does one build the Kingdom of God: bringing Him everywhere, without fear.

4

Father Amorth: The Plainspoken Priest
by Marcello Stanzione

Father Amantini and Padre Pio

Father Gabriele Amorth died September 16, 2016, at the age of ninety-one. He collaborated with Father Candido Amantini, a Passionist priest, at the Scala Sancta for a good six years, and at the death of Father Amantini, he became his successor; first, he was his alter ego and then his successor. This is how the disciple recalls his master:

> Father Candido Amantini was a Passionist, a man of God. St. Pio of Pietrelcina referred to him with a phrase that was then written on his tomb: "Father Candido is truly a priest according to the heart of God."

At times Padre Pio would send him some advice.

> Once Father Candido was exorcising a young man, and he said to me: "Look, Father Amorth, I was exorcising him like a Greco-Roman wrestling match, and I did not know who would be checked off. At times, there are people who are truly violent, and if a priest exorcist does not know ahead of time how to protect himself, for example, with

personal assistants, he could find himself in a bad way. In this case," he continued, "at a certain point, this young man collapsed, and I collapsed around him. And whoever might have witnessed it would not have understood who was the exorcist and who was the person being exorcised. Padre Pio sent me a note saying: 'Dear Father, it is useless for you to waste time and effort with that young man. There is nothing that can be done!' And I asked him: Why? He said the young man was an impenitent womanizer. He did not try to conquer his vice, and when one lives habitually in a state of sin, the exorcisms do not count for anything."

Father Amorth's Dramatic First Exorcism

Father Amorth's very first exorcism remained especially impressed in his mind. He spoke of it in various interviews and in his book *The Last Exorcist: My Battle against Satan*, in which he narrates in depth what happened with so many other important exorcisms.

His first solo exorcism (in 1997) was very particular, because he immediately clashed with Satan himself. After having assisted Father Candido Amantini for many years, he exorcised a simple peasant solo. The man was very young and slim and came accompanied by a priest and a third person, a translator. Initially, Father Amorth did not understand the reason for the translator, so the priest explained to him that when the demoniac was under possession, he spoke in English, and therefore it would be useful to have the translator present in order to understand what he was saying.

Once the exorcism began, the young peasant did not communicate with words or gestures; it was as if nothing affected him, not even when Father Amorth invoked the help of the Lord. But after the invocation, when the exorcist priest asked specifically for the help of Jesus, the young man fixed his gaze on him and began to yell in English. His curses and threats were aimed solely at the exorcist; then he began spitting at him and preparing to attack him physically; only when Father Amorth arrived at the prayer *Praecipio tibi* (I command you), did the demon seem to placate himself a bit. But then, screaming and howling, the demon burst forth and looked straight at him, drooling saliva from the young man's mouth. The exorcist, at that point, continued with the rite of liberation, asking and ordering the demon to tell him his name and reveal who he was.[9] Because this was his first exorcism, Father Amorth did not expect to receive such a terrifying response: "I am Lucifer." Thus, with great stupor, Father Amorth discovered that who he had in front of him in those moments was Lucifer in person, but at that point, he certainly could not give up or end the exorcism, so he engaged himself even more. He was convinced that he had to keep going as long as he had the strength.

So, while he continued with the prayers of liberation, the demon resumed his shrieks, making the possessed turn his head back and his eyes roll; and he remained like this with his back

---

[9] "Unclean spirit! Whoever you are and all your companions who possess this servant of God: By the mysteries of the Incarnation, the Sufferings and Death, the Resurrection, and the Ascension of Our Lord Jesus Christ; by the sending of the Holy Spirit; and by the Coming of Our Lord into the Last Judgment, I command you: Tell me, with some sign, your name, the day and the hour of your damnation. Obey me in everything, although I am an unworthy servant of God." "Summoning of the Evil Spirit," in *Roman Ritual of Exorcism*, 2.3.

arched for a quarter of an hour. Who could imagine what Father Amorth felt in those moments? Changes also occurred in the environment. All of a sudden, the room became extremely cold and ice crystals formed on the windows and the walls. The exorcist, refusing to give up, ordered Lucifer to abandon the peasant. But almost in response, the young man's body stiffened so much that he became hard and at a certain point began to levitate; and for several minutes, he remained hovering three feet in the air. Meanwhile, the exorcist continued with the prayers of liberation. Then, at a certain point, the possessed fell down onto a chair, and a little before disappearing, Lucifer announced the day and the exact hour that he would leave the body of the peasant.

Father Amorth continued to exorcise the young man each week until the fatal day arrived. Then he let another week pass, and he rescheduled him. Upon his arrival, the young man seemed very tranquil, and in the course of the exorcism, he did not make any objections to the liberations, and indeed, he prayed tranquilly. Father Amorth asked him to explain how Lucifer left him, and he replied that on the day and at the hour that the devil had indicated he would leave, he began to howl like never before. Then, at the end of this, he felt new and light.

Father Amorth Speaks of the Good Angels

Since exorcism must also be understood in the context of the good angels, Father Amorth wrote one of his columns in the weekly *Credo* on the good angels:

The angelic creatures who chose to remain faithful to their nature and to the goal for which they were created—that is, to praise God eternally—did a very simple thing: they remained obedient. They accepted being submissive to God the Creator, and they made their choice in the just view, not the diabolical view of feeling humiliated by this act of submission. To the contrary, in choosing to remain faithful to God, the angels were true to their nature and their end. It was an act of fidelity to the truth for which they were created by God, which is to love Him. This attitude does not humiliate them, because it does not infer a lack of something; rather, it reflects a fullness. The angels have continued to be faithful to their nature, which refers them directly to God the Creator, the one who has inscribed in creation the laws that He considers best for the good of the creature. Thus, the way we read it in the book of Revelation (12:7 and further on) is the way it occurred. There was a giant war between the angels who remained faithful to God and those who rebelled against Him; in other words, the [good] angels against the demons. In those passages, the Bible tells us that the Archangel Michael led the angels into battle, and the rebel angels were guided by the dragon (the devil) and at the end were defeated. As a result, and I cite from memory, "for them there was no longer a place in heaven."

Something happened here that the Bible does not declare, but that I have no reason to doubt: the demons created hell—that is, they put themselves in a situation, in a state, that placed them in opposition to God, and in doing so, harmed themselves. Their new condition, known in the Bible as "hell," means that the devils are forever excluded from paradise—that is, the vision of God, and the goals of enjoyment and eternal happiness for which they were created. Therefore, the demons are definitively condemned; for them, there is no longer any possibility of salvation. Why?

Because their intelligence, which is much superior to ours, since they are pure spirits, makes their choice definitive, because it was done with full awareness and is therefore not retractable. But the demons do not wish to take back such a choice. The same is true, but to the contrary, for the angels who have chosen God and enjoy Him in eternity; and it is also true for the saints, those who are already admitted to the eternal vision of God. And this is true also for us, who are called to sanctity here on earth and, if necessary, in purgatory.

How the Demon Enters Souls

The journalist Marco Tosatti asked Father Amorth which are the paths preferred by the devil when entering the soul of men. Amorth responded:

> There are four methods the demon utilizes to enter souls; one regards saints, and two are extremely rare. When the demon tempts a person who seems holy, he attempts to make him renounce his godly ways. This case is extremely rare. The other extremely rare case is that of leading a person into a complex of extremely serious sins in a way that is nearly irreversible. In my view, this was the method [that Satan used] with Judas Iscariot.... The most frequent case — and I put it at 90 percent — is that of the evil spell. It happens when someone sustains an evil caused by the demon that has been provoked by some person who has turned to Satan or someone who has acted with satanic perfidy. The remaining, 10 to 15 percent — I do not have an exact number — regard persons who have participated in occult practices, such as séances or satanic sects, or have contacted wizards and fortune-tellers. These

forms of Satanism are widely diffused, and I think that today they are spread by stars and celebrities who have a huge following, such as Marilyn Manson and other satanic rock musical groups. I have nothing against rock music; it is very respectable music; I am against satanic rock."[10]

Many in the Church Doubt the Reality of Satan

One of the first actions the Church must take up is to recognize the existence of such phenomena; today there is a tendency among philosophers and theologians to think that neither demons nor hell exist.[11] Father Gabriele Amorth supported this opinion during an interview:

Everyone speaks of Satan except the Church.[12]

Satan's greatest success is to make humanity believe that he does not exist, and he has nearly succeeded. Even in the Church: we have a clergy and an episcopate that no longer believes in the devil, in exorcisms, in extraordinary evils caused by the devil, and not even in the powers that Jesus gave to cast out demons. For three centuries, the Latin Church, in contrast to the Orthodox and various Protestant confessions, has nearly completely abandoned the ministry of exorcism. Since the Church is no longer practicing exorcisms and no longer studying them, and most clergy have not ever seen them, they no longer

[10] M. Tosatti: *Inquiry on the Devil* (Piemme: Casale Monferrato, 2003), p. 31.

[11] M. Moronta Rodriguez, "Pastoral Attitudes regarding the Phenomena of Satanism," *Religions and Sects in the World* (May 1992): 116.

[12] Tosatti, *Inquiry*, 181.

believe in them. There are entire nations deprived of exorcisms, such as Germany, Austria, Switzerland, Spain, and Portugal. It is a frightening absence.[13]

Father Amorth Explains How Priests Should Dress

In a book interview, the journalist Angela Musolesi asks Father Amorth what he thinks of the ecclesiastical habit:

You are always dressed as a priest, in both private and public encounters. Aside from obedience to the dispositions of canon law, are there other motives for which you always dress as a priest?

I share what Father Mariano said: it is very true that the habit does not make the monk, but it is also true that the habit tells you who is a monk. I might add, it forces you to behave in a manner consistent with the habit. It is for this reason that I always wear the habit, which I love, and also it clearly defines me; and I am immediately recognized as a priest.

Has it ever happened that a priest who does not wear any sign of priestly recognition is influenced by your practice of wearing the priestly habit?

Oh yes, there are many cases because today priests who do not wear any sign of their priesthood are the great majority.

Father Amorth Speaks of His Early Life

In a book interview with the Vaticanist Marco Tosatti, Father Amorth offers an autobiographical sketch:

---

[13] Stefano Maria Paci, "... E liberaci dal maligno" (And deliver us from evil), interview with Father Gabriele Amorth, Inter Multiplices Una Vox, http://www.unavox.it/ArtDiversi/div014.

I was born into a religious family. My parents and my four brothers, all much better than I, were all extremely religious. We received our religious formation in the family and from Catholic Action in the parish. We were formed at Modena, in the church of St. Peter, where now there is a Benedictine, my friend and one of the two exorcists of Modena.

My entire youth was a life of intensive religiosity. I spent all my youth in Catholic Action as a catechist, along with other activities. Around my fourteenth year, I began to think about my vocation; and then my dearest friend became a priest. We were schoolmates and graduated from the same classical high school, and everyone knew that he would become a priest. I think that he also influenced me in this matter. Okay, a priest, but where do I go? This was a problem. By a fortuitous chance, I had the opportunity to meet Father Giacomo Alberione, and he truly convinced me that he was a man of God. I asked him where I should enter the priesthood, in which congregation, which institution. He said to me: "Tomorrow morning I shall celebrate Mass for you." I got up early, because he celebrated mass at 4:00 a.m. "Ah, you are here," he said. After the Mass, he told me that I would enter the Society of St. Paul. I was in my second year of high school. I said: "Okay. I shall finish high school, then I shall enter." After high school, there was the war, but we always remained in contact with one another.

During the war, all five siblings were drafted into the army. We all had our own adventures. I participated in the war (the civil war) as a partisan; I experienced some hair-raising adventures, and I also received the medal of military valor. I thought, and I shared it with Father Alberione, that I should not leave the family during the war. I also asked him what I should choose as a major at the university. He said: "Choose whatever you wish."

I had two brothers who had law degrees, and I followed the same path. And I did well, because they gave me the degree as a gift. I did not study; I never attended class, because, out of the esteem they had toward my two brothers, they just passed me. And I graduated on schedule. Then in 1947, at the age of twenty-two, I enrolled in the Christian Democrat Party. I did not wish to do so, but I was pushed into it by our leader, Giuseppe Dossetti. He was my professor of canon and ecclesiastical law, and he was extremely close friends with my family. He came many times to dine and sleep at our house. He pushed every one of us to work in politics.

Our leader in Modena was Ermanno Gorrieri, a great friend from my school days. Good, humble, but full of enterprise, he was our leader during the partisan war; he was also the leader of our section of the Christian Democrats, which we founded. I organized sections of the Christian Democrats in many places in Lower Modena, something of which no one had ever heard of. And this made me feel a little like my father, who had been a friend of Don Sturzo[14] and was a founder at Modena of the Popular Party (Partito Popolare Italiano). At the first elections of the Provincial Council, I was immediately elected. And at the fiftieth anniversary, the secretary of the Christian Democrat Party, Ciriaco De Mita, came to grant us rewards for having founded the party fifty years ago and for our service, especially De Mita, who had been a prime minister of Italy.

Then I was sent—prompted by Dossetti—to be the national vice delegate of the Christian Democratic Youth, which was

---

[14] Father Luigi Sturzo (1891–1959), born in Caltagirone, Sicily, was a political leader and founder, in 1919, of the Italian People's Party (PPI).

then very influential. I went to Rome for a few months. The [chief] delegate was Giulio Andreotti, and then there was me. I did everything alone, because Andreotti dedicated all his time to De Gasperi. He left all the youth groups to me. And when he was nominated the first time as undersecretary to the president of the Council, he resigned his post as national delegate to the Christian Democratic Youth. I understood that they would have nominated me national delegate; and I also understood that if I got further involved with politics, I would have never left it. So I took advantage of the moment to set myself free.

I had remained in contact with Father Alberione. I knew that he had made a vow to Our Lady: that if all the members of the Pauline family survived the war safely, he would build a sanctuary to Our Lady, Queen of the Apostles. And he built it, here, three vertical sanctuaries, one above the other — not three churches, but three sanctuaries. I knew of this plan, and I asked him: "Include me and my brothers, we five, among your sons protected by Our Lady during the war." We five had had some adventures! One of my brothers who is still living returned on foot from Karlovac in Yugoslavia. All of us had our adventures and misadventures, but all were saved.

I shall always remember the day I became a priest; the day of the ordination was January 24 of 1954. The ordination had been pushed forward because Father Alberione wished to have us ordained in the centenary of the dogma of the Immaculate Conception. After the Mass and the photographs, the new priests, with their families, went to Father Alberione's office to greet him. I also went with my four brothers and my mother. And he immediately asked me: "How did all of you get by during the war?" He remembered very well the promise he had made to include me and my brothers in his prayer for protection to the Queen of the Apostles. It was then that I realized it was Jesus who said to Father Alberione that I must enter the Society of St. Paul, and I have never regretted it.

Another Interview with Father Amorth

As an exorcist, Father Amorth was always considered a great chatterbox, because he always spoke frankly and openly. I report here an interview Father Gabriele released years ago during a course for exorcists in Rome at the university Regina Apostolorum.

Could you tell us something regarding special charisms, especially that of prophecy?

Prophecy is not truly demonstrable because there are people who have some natural gifts of foresight, which have no particular relationship to God or to the action of a demon. I would say that we have not treated the problem of those who have particular charisms, but any confirmations would have to be convincing.

Regarding charismatics, must we entrust ourselves to them or use prudence?

It is extremely wise to be on guard for false charismatics! There are many of them! I entrust myself to a certain charismatic because I know that his bishop trusts him, and I have known him for many years. I also know that he is not infallible. But I can say that very often he arrives at the truth. He is the only charismatic I trust.

Regarding sensitives, are there some signs that can make us understand if they are good or not?

When these sensitives are persons of prayer and truly humble, they try to remain hidden; these are the positive signs. But if a person says, "I am a charismatic," then he has no charism. The charismatic is humble and has hidden gifts that God gives him. The Lord would give many more charisms if there was more faith. I think of *Lumen Gentium* of Vatican II, which says in paragraph 12: "Those who have charge over the Church [bishops] should judge the genuine and orderly use of these gifts, and it is especially [the role of] their office not indeed to extinguish the Spirit, but to test all things and hold fast to what is good" (see 1 Thess. 5:12, 19–21).

Is the exorcist infallible in his judgment or in his ministry?

I have had various cases of persons who, before turning to me, went to numerous exorcists without gaining any benefit. After coming to me, they said that they attained some benefits. In the same way, other persons who came to me several times did not gain any improvements and found success with other exorcists. It is the Holy Spirit who commands! It is not the one who plants and cultivates; it is the Lord who causes growth. So, the invocation to the Holy Spirit is the prayer that must never be lacking. Other things are useless.

Is it possible for demons to tempt those at the summit of the Church, the hierarchy?

The devil assails those at the summits, all of the summits: politics, sports, media, and social life in general, but in a particular way, those at the summits of the Church! It is well known, unfortunately, that in the Vatican there are persons who are solely careerists; those who are seeking only the things below, not those above; and the devil profits from this, dazzling those who seek success and power. The devil assails those at the summit of the Church, the center of Christian life. It is not said that he always succeeds. But where there are persons interacting, there are always human weaknesses.

Regarding Monsignor Milingo, do you think that he was a victim of the devil?[15]

I believe that Monsignor Milingo was unduly influenced or taken by something strange. But I am not sure of it. After the first dismissal, he returned to the Church. He loved John Paul II, and it was with reference to John Paul's request that he reentered the ecclesial communion. But he continued to have contact with Moon and his followers. Monsignor Milingo, as a good African, was very tied to Africa, and he wished to help. Moon and his followers gave much money to Milingo, which he sent to Africa to build hospitals, schools, et cetera. This was the reason he remained in contact with the followers of Moon at Zagarolo (a town south of Rome). He was never completely detached from them. I do not wish to say anything more.

Can one force a person to be exorcised?

One cannot make a person submit to an exorcism if he does not wish to from the beginning. There have been cases where people came to me saying: "Look, Father, I came here solely because my parents wish to have me see you. But I do not want you to do an exorcism on me." Then I give the person a blessing, nothing more, if he accepts it. If, at the beginning of the rite, a person who has asked for an exorcism begins, at the last moment, to

---

[15] Emmanuel Milingo was appointed archbishop of Zambia in 1969 by Paul VI. In 2001, he received a marriage blessing from Sun Myung Moon, the leader of the Unification Church. After some back-and-forth, on December 17, 2009, he was reduced to the lay state, making him no longer a member of the clergy.

oppose it with great resistance, then, in that case, one can "force one's hand." Some people come to me who are forcefully pushed to enter my room. It has also happened that once they arrive, they do not wish to get out of the car. Then I get into the car, and I do the exorcism in the car. These persons wish to have the exorcisms; it is the demon that is impeding them from reaching the exorcist. In those cases, one can force the person, even with force, to accept the exorcism. It is necessary, however, to have the consent of the family, those who are bringing the subject to the exorcist.

I also have had cases in which the person does not wish to be exorcised but afterward is content. But, be aware that many of these persons need years of exorcisms to arrive at liberation! St. Alphonsus Liguori said: "One is not always able to liberate a person from diabolical possession. But one is always able to give some relief." I have exorcised some persons for fifteen or twenty years, who have made some great progress, but they are not yet liberated. But there has often been some great progress in their families. I remember a woman who was exorcised for many years by Father Candido. Then I exorcised her. She is still not free. I remember thinking that it is useless because I always find myself at the same point. But the woman said to me: "We are a large family, with many siblings. Not one of us went to church, and no one prayed. Since I have had this disturbance, all my brothers and sisters and their families pray and go to Mass." We look for immediate results in the world, while the Lord looks at eternal life. It is providential, therefore, that this person has been struck; this disturbance has brought all of her family into the Church, making them practice again. There are then persons who offer themselves as victims. At times, they ask the Lord not to liberate them. I think of a nun who was possessed by the devil and was never liberated. She offered all her tremendous suffering for the souls in purgatory, for the conversion of sinners, and for her spiritual children, the same goals Jesus had when dying on the Cross. All these sufferings offered to God have great value.

If, when hands are imposed during the prayer of liberation, a person manifests reactions that give the impression there is a possession, and the person is not exorcised, what should the person do?

If the person is in a trance, one can continue with the prayer of liberation. But in the end, the priest must recommend to the person in question to go to an exorcist so that he can examine the situation.

Concerning this, it is necessary to note that symptoms that a psychiatrist identifies as a psychic illness are different from those that an exorcist concludes is an evil presence. The help of the psychiatrist is useful, provided that each one knows how to remain in his own field. The psychiatrist cannot say: "You have an illness that I am not able to identify, that I cannot cure." In the same way, an exorcist cannot say: "You are schizophrenic." Rather, the exorcist can say: "I cannot find in you any evil presence." Each one has to remain in his own field.

When a priest finds himself in a group and, all of a sudden, someone manifests some supernatural reality, perhaps even a possession, can he proceed with an exorcism? I am thinking of a priest who has not been appointed an exorcist and does not have the immediate possibility of contacting his bishop.

If the priest is not an exorcist—that is, he does not have the faculty or authority from his bishop to do exorcisms—then he cannot do exorcisms. He must limit himself to saying prayers of liberation. But I say that everyone can say prayers of liberation, as reported by the evangelical passage of Mark: "These signs will accompany those who believe: in my name they will cast out demons" (Mark 16:17). Therefore, the fundamental condition for casting out the demon is faith, even the faith of a baby or a child.

There is the famous case of an exorcist who lived at the time of St. Catherine of Siena. When he was not able to liberate a person, he would send him to the saint, and she would liberate him.

But the priest who does not have the explicit permission of the bishop cannot do the exorcism, that is, recite the prayers of the Ritual reserved for the exorcists. But he can do the prayers of liberation. And if he does them with faith, they are very efficacious. The groups of the Catholic Charismatic Renewal come to mind; those groups that pray the prayers of liberation often obtain the liberation of the person from the demon. Many saints have liberated persons from the demon, without being exorcists and, at times, without even being priests. St. Benedict was not a priest or an exorcist. He was a monk, a saint. Although he was never declared the patron of the exorcists, he is considered as such. His medal is worn everywhere! He liberated many people from demonic possession with prayer.

The curricula in the seminaries are a bit lacking regarding the formation of exorcists. How, then, are exorcists trained?

It is important that the seminaries return to the study of the ascetic and mystical theologies, the subjects that, among others, address how questions concerning problems with the demons, possessions, and exorcisms are treated, so that the new priest is instructed at least in theory in these matters. I also advise, from a practical point of view, that when a priest is preparing to become an exorcist, other than the theoretical study of books on these topics, he needs to observe and assist an exorcist. From the observation of the concrete exorcistical practice, one learns how it is done and how one must act. This is the true, practical school that helps a priest to prepare for this ministry.

Is there such a thing as a school that prepares a priest to become an exorcist?

The school of exorcism is practical experience. Once there were so many exorcists. The exorcist was one among many other priests. When one could no longer work, another exorcist was prepared to replace him. Then there was the tremendous period for which, for three centuries, in the Latin Church, exorcisms were interrupted. It was a period that I call bestial, in which persons, rather than being exorcised, were accused of being witches and sent to the stake. After three centuries of exaggerations, the belief in the devil diminished or disappeared in the three successive centuries. Exorcisms were no longer done. This is why they were no longer spoken of in the seminaries. The devil was no longer spoken of; the struggle between the angels and demons was no longer spoken of; diabolical possessions were no longer spoken of; and as a result, we have a clergy that no longer believes in any of these things. New bishops are chosen from among these priests, and so not even the bishops believe. They have never studied or ever seen exorcisms. They have never exercised this ministry.

Where can one go for an apprenticeship, in order to become an exorcist?

One must turn to an exorcist in one's diocese. If there is not an exorcist in the diocese, one must turn to another diocese. For example, the dean of exorcists, near San Giovanni Rotondo, can indicate the names of exorcists in particular dioceses. [Concerning all the other dioceses, I do not know.] Father La Grua (who died in Palermo in 2012) and Father Benigno in Sicily, who, on behalf of the Sicilian episcopate, gathered the exorcists of Sicily to offer them instruction, knew the exorcists of various dioceses. [Those who have this information] can then indicate the names of the exorcists of the various areas. In Italy, one can find exorcists even though they are much engaged. I myself, in Rome, am swamped with appointments and engagements.

When you were appointed an exorcist, was it for a brief time?
At that time, when one was appointed an exorcist, he was given the authority to do exorcisms *sine die* (indefinitely). The exorcist could then be retired. But if he was not retired, he could continue. I have done exorcisms for twenty-three years and no one has withdrawn the authority. So I proceed with my ministry. Currently, one uses the faculty or authority for a year and then, when it expires, renews it.

Once a bishop nominates an exorcist, must the nominated priest assist an experienced exorcist?
There is no doubt that preparation is important. I'll make a comparison with medicine. A student of medicine studies in depth the hernia operation, or the appendix operation, which are basic surgical procedures. Do you then entrust yourself to that person to go "under the knife"? I think not! After having studied the matter, it is necessary for that person to assist another surgeon until he has enough practical experience to do the surgical procedures by himself. The school for exorcists also consists of assisting another exorcist. I assisted at the exorcisms of Father Candido Amantini. Then I did the exorcisms with him, and finally I did

them by myself. This is how. One becomes an exorcist by working with an expert exorcist, not solely studying from books.

In some charismatic groups, the laity also imposes or lays on hands. Is this correct?

I am contrary to the imposition of hands on the part of the laity, because it is a typically priestly gesture. Unless there are particular circumstances; for example, a father or a mother who imposes hands on their child saying a prayer. This is more than legitimate. But what is this mania of laying on hands during the prayers of liberation, on the head or the shoulders? No! It is not necessary to touch during the prayers of liberation! I am opposed to these ways.

How does the exorcist choose his assistants?

The exorcist must be very careful in the choice of his assistants; he must know them well. Some priests ask me if they can assist at my exorcisms, but I say no if I do not know them. I wish to know first if they are persons of prayer, of faith.

How much does the prayer of the laity matter?

Each one relies on his personal experiences. I think of Father Matteo La Grua, who was the principal exorcist of Sicily. He, as a good member of the Renewal of the Spirit, had the gift of speaking in tongues. I sometimes participated at his exorcisms when he spoke in tongues. Then he used the Ritual. He liked to have prayer groups but not where he was doing exorcisms; rather, he would have them accompany him in prayer before the Blessed Sacrament. He was very demanding with these persons. It is very useful to be helped by prayer groups, both the consecrated religious (men and women), and lay groups. The laity can also help very much with their prayers, even without being present at the exorcisms. I ask for prayers from family members, friends, and others who are accompanying the one I am subjecting to exorcisms. I ask them to pray for the success of the exorcisms that I am doing. This prayer is precious.

What can be the role of the psychiatrist?

When an exorcist finds himself in doubt as to whether a person is a demoniac or suffering from a psychic disorder, he needs the help of the psychiatrist. It is also possible, at times, that a person suffers contemporaneously a diabolical possession and a psychic illness, for which it is possible that he needs the psychiatrist and the exorcist. In certain cases, the presence of the psychiatrist is also useful to the exorcist, because some cases are very difficult to diagnose. But the exorcist is also useful to the psychiatrist. I have had various cases sent to me by psychiatrists. I think of a nun who is still struck by a diabolical possession. A Catholic psychiatrist understood that he needed an exorcist, given that his science was not helping to explain the problem.

I am a medical doctor. What do you recommend that I do to help these persons?

Prayer is useful for everything. I have read so many treatises by various authors. I think of a cardiologist from the United States who divided his department in two: in one part, his patients received his treatment, and he prayed for them. Those in the other part also received his treatment, but he did not pray for them. And he noted a very great advantage on the part of patients for whom he prayed, other than curing them. I have read so many examples like this. I would say that prayer, the union with God, is extremely important. Invite your patients to pray much, in order to make their therapies effective and your diagnosis correct. Prayer is also important in accompanying a medical intervention.

Which prayers of liberation are the most efficacious?

I have noted that the most effective prayers of liberation are those of praise and gratitude to God. The Ritual also advises praying the psalms of praise to God. The prayers of praise to God are much more efficacious than pronouncing phrases such as: "In the name of Jesus, Satan, go away!" because one is thanking and praising God, who works the liberation and the cure. So we must emphasize prayers of praise and glory to God, because these prayers are very efficacious.

Can lay members of Pentecostal movements turn to the demon during a prayer of liberation to ask his name or another question?

The Congregation for the Doctrine of the Faith (CDF) prohibits asking the demon his name. I believe that this is extended to everyone. No one should dialogue with the demon, even if he tries to begin a dialogue with the laity who are reciting the prayer of liberation. For example, in the Acts of the Apostles, when some Jewish exorcists turn to the demon, telling him: "I adjure you by the Jesus whom Paul preaches," the evil spirit replies, "Jesus I know, and Paul I know; but who are you?" And then the demon hurls himself at them, wounding them and stripping them (Acts 19:13–16). If one does not have the protection that the exorcists have — the Church — it is necessary to be extremely prudent and not begin any dialogue with the demon! Although the CDF document explicitly prohibits asking the name, I believe it is appropriate to exclude any dialogue with the demon precisely because one does not have the authority that the exorcist has been given by the Church, which guarantees his protection in these circumstances.

In the Gospel of Mark, one reads: "These signs will accompany those who believe: in my name they will cast out demons; they will speak in new tongues" (16:17). Men, women, young people, adults, laymen, and priests can all pray prayers of liberation. It is a private prayer authorized by Jesus, and no bishop may prohibit it. And if some bishop attempts to prohibit it, as has happened, we must say: "It is better to obey God than men" (see Acts 5:29). Their order is invalid. The exorcism—that is, a sacramental, a public prayer done in the name of the Church that involves the authority of the Church—is stronger per se. But when a person who is far away asks me for help and there is no exorcist nearby authorized by the bishop (as happens in countries such as France, Germany, and Portugal and in Latin America), I am the first to urge them to go to a priest who says the prayers of healing and liberation, prayers that all priests can legitimately say. It would be a good thing if all priests recited them, but this does not always happen, simply because many priests do not believe in them. Or I recommend that such people go to the groups of the [Charismatic] Renewal, where they say prayers of healing and liberation, which are private prayers but, when done with faith, are of great efficacy. Also, a priest's blessing has a great effect, but the priests do not know it and do not believe it.

Regarding Masses of healing, how are prayers of liberation formulated?

Before beginning the celebration of a [healing] Mass, it is necessary to advise the faithful that it is possible that during the Mass someone may cry out, fall to the floor, et cetera. For this reason, and also because each of the faithful has the right to participate at the Mass peacefully, without interruptions, these prayers are usually recited at the end of the function so that the time necessary for meditation and silence is respected. If someone cries out, I ask them to leave. But that does not mean no one will howl, shriek, et cetera. In the Masses of healing and liberation that I celebrate in Florence, episodes of this kind occur. But the faithful know it. During these prayer encounters, I recall some of these persons coming to receive Communion and throwing themselves on the floor; so [after a while] I decided I did not want them anymore because it is difficult to maintain discipline during these so-called healing Masses. I say: "so-called" because all Masses are healing and liberating. When Jesus is present, all the Masses are healing and liberating. But when, during the Mass, one intends to say some particular prayers of healing and liberation, it is necessary to alert the faithful in advance.

What is your opinion of homeopathy and Reiki?

One cannot equate homeopathy with Reiki. Reiki of course is condemned. Homeopathy, when it is done with competence, is an alternative to official medicine and has the right to be looked at with respect and used with respect. I know many persons who are treated advantageously with homeopathic medicine. There is no danger when it is utilized by competent medical doctors and specialists, because it is only a treatment based on herbs—that is, on natural materials. Therefore, homeopathy is respectable.

What are the real risks for exorcists?

I would say that, in substance, there are no risks for exorcists, as long as the exorcist lives a life of prayer. An exorcist may risk becoming a braggart; therefore, he must always consider himself an instrument of God, because the one who renders the exorcism effective is the Lord, not the good intention or the engagement of the exorcist. I have known exorcists who pretend to have some charisms and who say things that they make up. The exorcist must maintain a life of prayer and humility, under the protection of Jesus and Mary. Only in this way can the exorcist be tranquil and carry out the mission entrusted to him by the Church, to the advantage of the faithful and without harm to himself.

Who can be struck by the demon? Can the demon strike an exorcist?

Anyone can be struck by the demon, with the exception of the one who prays or who lives in the grace of God. Father Candido said to me: "Think of how we exorcists are battered by evil spells! Yet they do nothing to us; they do not touch us! We are protected by God and by the angels."

While Cardinal Poletti was writing the decree for my nomination, I was recommending myself to Our Lady: "Wrap me in your mantle." So many times, the demons have said: "We can do nothing to you because you are too protected."

We can say, in general, that everyone can be the object of evil actions. But, for the one who prays, who is close to God and who lives in the grace of God, the situation is different; he is protected. This generates a type of boomerang effect: many wizards are afraid of the evil spells because they fear that they will fall on themselves.

Can the exorcist modify parts of the Ritual?

The exorcist can, with the permission of the bishop, utilize the old or the new Ritual. I add also that the exorcist, before proceeding with the rite, must take into account the person to whom he must administer the exorcism. For this reason, I would say, there are no two exorcists alike. Exorcists acquire some practices that, according to their experience, are effective. These are not always shared by all the other exorcists. One example: the invocation of the saints. I recall the case of the dean of exorcists, Father Cipriano, an exorcist for fifty years and vice postulator for the cause of his confrere Brother Matthew. When Father Cipriano invoked the intercession of this confrere, toward whom he nurtured a great veneration, the demon that he was exorcizing would become infuriated! Many times, the exorcist invokes this or that saint's intercession; or, at other times, he makes use of relics. On the basis of his own faith, and the faith of the one who is being exorcized, he receives some verification with respect to the efficacy of these invocations. Therefore, we can also say that the exorcist has a certain liberty of action in conducting the exorcism. He does not have to keep strictly to the official text of the Ritual to reach liberation.

What can we do to be sure that the possessed person has experienced liberation? Must the prayers of exorcism continue after liberation?

I have always feared being before bogus or provisional liberations, cases in which the demon pretends to have gone away. The fear is such that it pushes me to postpone the prayer of gratitude until at least a year after the liberation. In these cases, one must recommend that the person liberated not desist from all that he has done in order to reach liberation: not to desist from prayer and from approaching the sacraments, and thus remain close to God. Indeed, the great risk is that the demon will pretend to have gone away from the possessed, inducing the person, a little at a time, to reduce his pious practices, and, thus fall back into what God does not wish: a life of sin. It is in these circumstances that relapses occur that are comparable to the mention in the Gospel of the [evil] spirit that leaves a soul, goes away, then wanders around, saying: "I shall return to my home from which I came," and he returns with seven other spirits worse than him, making the situation of that soul worse than before (Matt. 12:43–45). I also had some cases—extremely rare, thank heaven—of persons who, once liberated, neglected their prayer life a little at a time and fell back into a life of sin. Let us not forget that when the demon enters a person, he does not abandon him; indeed, he does everything he can to be able to return.

Is it possible to carry around blessed water or even a consecrated Host?

A priest can have the consecrated Host and blessed water with him in order to do prayers of liberation on a home, for single individuals, and above all for the ill. There is no prohibition against a priest having a consecrated Host on his person. I confess to you: I have the Eucharist here with me right now. I always have the Eucharist with me, even when I do exorcisms. There is no prohibition.

Could you say something about the use of sacramentals in exorcisms? I am referring to water, oil, and blessed salt.

Some sacramentals, such as the imposition of hands and blessed oil and salt, have always been used during exorcisms, unlike blessed water, which entered into use more recently. It is important to emphasize that these three sacramentals act like all sacramentals, according to the power of faith. Whereas the sacraments act ipso facto, sacramentals are efficacious solely if used for and with faith. For this reason, it is important that the faithful know how to use the sacramentals correctly. It makes no sense to keep large quantities of blessed water, salt, and blessed oil if one does not have faith. Each sacramental [used during an exorcism] has its own characteristics. The prayer in Latin clarifies their meaning. These three sacramentals are used to liberate us from the influence of the demon. The blessed salt, for example, gives special protection to places. Father Candido recommended putting a little bit of blessed salt in a room that is considered infested.

The blessed oil has the power to cure ills and chase demons. During an exorcism, I use the first Ritual, which includes the possibility of anointing the possessed with oil. I anoint the five senses: the forehead, eyes, nostrils, throat, mouth and ears, tracing on the possessed the Sign of the Cross. I repeat, a gesture must be done with faith in order to be effective. Two Russian saints—whose names I do not recall—chased demons by anointing [the afflicted] with blessed oil. They were not exorcists. They did not use the Ritual. But they were saints; they prayed, and they chased the demons.

Blessed water is used for blessing places and persons. One can also drink blessed water, but with faith, taking little sips. Some of the principal effects are liberation from the snares of the Evil One and protection from him. Also, for us exorcists, it is worth recalling Christ's announcement: "Those who believe: in my name they will cast out demons." Consequently, if a priest has the authority to do exorcisms and to act in the name of the Church, it is because he has faith. When I find myself administering an exorcism, I always ask the Holy Spirit to come to my aid. Without Him, my intervention would be fruitless.

I know a woman whose husband does not believe that she is possessed. It would seem that the possession is in some way provoked by the husband's mother. How do you confront the incredulity of the husband?

This situation occurs frequently: jealous mothers view the daughter-in-law — especially when there is an only son — as an enemy who is taking her beloved son from her. Very often the mothers-in-law become intrusive; they interfere in everything. In the worst cases, they order evil spells to the disadvantage of the daughters-in-law. I have exorcised many women whose spells were wished by their mothers-in-law.

Concerning the case in question, to attain the liberation of the possessed wife, it would be necessary to persuade the husband to go to church and to pray et cetera.

Have you ever been subjected to a "joke" on the part of the devil?

I recall an episode. Once, after much time exorcising a person, the demon began mocking me. He said he would abandon the person on December 8, the feast of the Immaculate Conception. That day, for the first and only time, helped by Father Giacobbe, I did an exorcism for five and a half hours. At the end, the possessed seemed to be liberated! There were tears, embraces, and immense satisfaction. I recall going to my confreres and saying: "We liberated a person from the devil!" But after a week, we were back where we were before the exorcism. Father Candido said: "It is useless to do long exorcisms. It does not serve any purpose!" I asked the demon why he did not go away on that day, and he responded: "Don't you know that I am a liar?" I can assure you that I felt humiliated by that demon!

Do you believe that Freemasonry is a type of satanic lobby?

Unfortunately, Freemasonry is extremely widespread in our times. Freemasonry is the major support of satanic sects. The stealing of Hosts and ciboriums is often organized by the masons. They pay very well. Some years ago, a young girl informed me that they paid up to fifty dollars each time you brought them the consecrated Host. A satanic mass cannot be celebrated without the profanation of a consecrated Host. Consequently, I always repeat that the Freemasons and all who dedicate themselves to satanic masses or to Satanism believe in the Real Presence of Jesus in the Eucharist! If not, they would not make so much effort to gain possession of consecrated Hosts.

What do you advise when satanic molestation is caused by cursing, for example, in a home among the family?

I advise many prayers of reparation! When one has the vice of cursing, it is difficult to abandon it. Sometimes one succeeds. The person who happens to hear a curse can say a prayer and do some acts of reparation.

Devotion to Our Lady
by Marcello Stanzione and Father Amorth

Father Amorth's Marian devotion

Father Amorth affirmed in an interview:

> Generally, I invoke Our Lady of the Immaculate Conception, the Mother of God. I am also devoted to the appellation Our Lady of Guadalupe, the Madonna who converted Latin America, which otherwise would not have been converted. Before Our Lady, there were missionaries, who obtained nothing. When she came, she appeared as an Aztec, so the locals felt that she was one of their own, not a figure imported from across the ocean. Through Our Lady, God arrived, and they converted.
>
> I am very close to Our Lady of Guadalupe because, in the ancient Indian language, the name Guadalupe means "the one who crushed the head of the serpent." To me, this indicates that Our Lady of Guadalupe is the protector of all those who practice my ministry.

In 1942, on the occasion of the vocational visit of Father Alberione, the young Gabriele asked him to be included, with his family, in the vow that the future beatified made to Our Lady at the start of World War II: that he would construct a sanctuary dedicated to Our Lady if no member of the Pauline Family died in the war.

At that time, the Society of St. Paul included priests and four congregations for women. Thus it happened that all were saved, and after the war, Father Alberione kept his promise and ordered the construction of the sanctuary dedicated to Our Lady, Queen of the Apostles; today it is the Marian center of the Pauline Family throughout the world. In this sanctuary, on Monday, September 19, [2016], the funeral of Father Amorth was celebrated. Both Father Amorth and his mother, Josephine, were always convinced that their family was protected precisely by this vow.

Father Gabriele was very devoted to Mary, whom the Paulines venerate as Our Lady, Queen of the Apostles. Each morning, he prayed all the mysteries of the Rosary. It is significant that one of his last books (*Il Mio Rosario*) was dedicated to the practice of the Rosary, a prayer to which he was always devoted and which he recommended to the troubled persons of his exorcistic ministry.

Father Amorth Interviewed about His Marian Devotion

Some years ago, on Radio Maria Father Amorth described his devotion to Mary:

I have for many months written a column for the monthly *Eco of Medjugorje*, entitled The Woman, the Enemy of Satan. The inspiration came to me through the continuous references in Our Lady's messages regarding Satan; for example: Satan is strong, he is very bad, he is always in ambush, he acts when prayer is neglected, he puts us in his hands without reflecting, he obstructs our path to sanctity, he wishes to destroy God's plans, he wishes to defeat Mary's projects, he wishes to take first place in our life, he wishes to take away our joy. These diabolic actions are conquered through prayer, fasting, vigilance, and the Rosary.

In contrast to those who deny the devil's existence or minimize his actions, the Virgin Mary continually puts us on guard against him. It has never been difficult to relate the words attributed to Our Lady at Medjugorje to phrases in the Bible or the Magisterium. The Bible presents Mary to us as the enemy of Satan and shows us how to imitate her ways so that we may fulfill God's plan for us. Based on our experience, we exorcists can testify that the role of the Immaculate One is fundamental in the struggle against Satan.

The three encounters that I will reflect on here today reveal that Mary's presence and intervention are necessary to defeat Satan.

We encounter Mary's first appearance at the beginning of human history. In the book of Genesis, we are presented with a rebellion against God, a condemnation—but also a hope: the figure of Mary and of her Son will defeat the demon that was able to get the better of Adam and Eve. This is the first announcement of salvation; it is the Protevangelium,[16] which we find in Genesis 3:15.

In art, it is represented by the figure of Mary crushing the head of the serpent. In reality, on the basis of the sacred text, Jesus is "the progeny of the woman" who crushes the head of Satan. The Redeemer chose Mary not only as a mother, but also [as the one] associated with Him in the work of salvation. Therefore,

---

[16] Protevangelium: the earliest utterance of the gospel.

the configuration of the Virgin crushing the head of the serpent indicates these truths: Mary participated in the redemption, and Mary is the first fruit of that redemption.

At the end of human history, we [shall] find the same scene. In fact, the book of Revelation tells us that "a great portent appeared in heaven, a woman clothed with the sun, with the moon under her feet, and on her head a crown of twelve stars; she was with child and she cried out in her pangs of birth, in anguish for delivery. And another portent appeared in heaven; behold, a great red dragon, with seven heads and ten horns" (Rev. 12:1–3). The woman is Mary and she is giving birth to her son, Jesus, for whom she also represents the community of believers. It is unusual in the Bible to give multiple meanings to the same figure.

The red dragon is the ancient serpent, the devil or Satan. Again there is a struggle between the two figures, with the defeat of the dragon that falls to earth. For those of us who combat the demon, this enmity, struggle, and final result have great importance.

The second encounter with Mary in history is her role during her earthly life. I limit myself to some reflections on two accepted roles, Mary as Mother of God and Mary as our Mother. In the Annunciation, Mary demonstrates a total acceptance. The angel intervenes in her life and disrupts it beyond human imagination; and she responds with true faith, based solely on God's Word, for which nothing is impossible, not even a virgin giving birth. This faith, on the other hand, also highlights God's way of acting, as presented in *Lumen Gentium*: Mary was "used by God not merely in a passive way, but as freely cooperating in the work of human salvation through faith and obedience" (no. 56). With total faith and liberty, she carried out God's greatest plan, the Incarnation of the Word. " The Father of mercies willed that the Incarnation should be preceded by the acceptance of her who was predestined to be the mother of His Son, so that just as a woman contributed to death, so also a woman should contribute to life" (no. 56). The Eve-Mary comparison will be a very important theme to the early Fathers of the Church. The obedience of Mary, which helped to redeem the world, will herald the obedience of Christ, which would redeem the disobedience of Adam. Satan does not directly appear here, but the consequences of his intervention are being remedied.

The second annunciation occurs at the foot of the Cross, when Jesus says: "Woman, behold your son" (John 19:26). It is there that the availability of Mary and her faith and obedience are even stronger and more heroic than at the Annunciation. In order to understand this, we must direct our thoughts to the Virgins' feelings at that time: we immediately become aware that an immense love is being joined to a heartrending pain.

In addition to these emotions, we can add another three, for Mary and for us, and it is on these that I now wish to dwell.

The first is adhesion to the will of the Father. Vatican II uses a totally new expression when it tells us that, at the foot of the Cross, Mary was "lovingly consenting to the immolation of this Victim which she herself had brought forth" (*Lumen Gentium*, no. 58). What does this mean? If the Father wishes it like this, and Jesus accepted it like this; then she also, out of obedience, chooses to adhere to such a will, as painful as it may be.

The second sentiment—on which there is too little reflection and which is seemingly absurd to human understanding—is that the support of that sorrow, and every sorrow, is the understanding that, although humanly absurd, it is through that sorrow that Jesus triumphs, reigns, and wins. The Archangel Gabriel announced it to her in advance: "He will be great.... The Lord

God will give to him the throne of his father David, and he will reign over the house of Jacob for ever; and of his kingdom there will be no end" (Luke 1:32–33). So Mary understands that those prophecies of greatness will be accomplished through Christ's death on the Cross. The ways of God are not our ways (see Isa. 55:8); even less are the ways of Satan our ways.

The third sentiment that crowns all others is gratitude. In this sorrow, Mary sees the redemption of all mankind being carried out, and she understands that it was applied to her in advance; that it is through that atrocious death that all generations will call her blessed. As a result, all of us can look to heaven with certitude: in virtue of Jesus' death and Resurrection, the demon has definitively been defeated, and paradise is wide open. Each time we look at the crucifix, let us say thank you. It is through these sentiments: adhesion to the will of the Father, understanding the value of suffering, and faith in the victory of Christ through the cross that each one of us has the power to defeat Satan and to liberate ourselves if we fall into his possession.

The third topic I wish to reflect on is Mary, the enemy of Satan. Let us consider it in the way it was first presented. Let us also ask one another why Mary is so powerful against the demon and why the demon trembles and flees at the sight of the Virgin. Up to now, we have exposed the doctrinal motives, but it is time to say something more immediate, something that reflects the experience of exorcists.

The demon, when forced by God, speaks of Our Lady better than any preacher. In 1823 at Ariano Irpino (Campania) two celebrated Dominican preachers, Father Cassiti and Father Pignataro, were exorcising a boy. At the time, among theologians, the doctrine of the Immaculate Conception was still in the discussion stage: another thirty-one years would pass before it would be proclaimed a dogma of the faith (1854). The two priests ordered the demon to demonstrate that Mary was the Immaculate Conception and commanded him to do it through a sonnet. We must keep in mind that the demoniac was an illiterate twelve-year-old child. Satan immediately pronounced this verse:

> *I am the true Mother of God, who is my Son,*
> *And I am His daughter, although His Mother.*
> *He was born from eternity and is my Son.*
> *I was born within time, and yet I am His Mother,*
> *He is my Creator and is my Son.*
> *I am His creation and His mother.*
> *It was a divine marvel that my Son*
> *was an eternal God, who had me as His Mother.*
> *Our being is almost shared between Mother and Son,*
> *because the Mother received her existence from her Son,*
> *and the Son also received His existence from His Mother.*
> *If, then, the Son received His existence from His Mother,*
> *we either must say that the son was stained by the Mother,*
> *or we must say that the Mother is Immaculate.*

Pius IX was moved when, after having proclaimed the dogma of the Immaculate Conception, he read this sonnet; in fact, it was presented to him on that occasion.

Some years ago, a friend from Brescia, Father Faustino Negrini, was doing an exorcism near the small sanctuary of Our Lady of the Star and asked the demon: "Why do you have such terror of the Virgin Mary?" He heard his response through the demoniac: "Because she is the most humble of all and I am the most proud; because she is the most obedient and I am the most rebellious (toward God); and because she is the most pure and I am the vilest."

In 1991, while I was exorcizing a demoniac, I recalled this episode, and I repeated the words said in honor of Mary by the demon and, without having the slightest idea what he would have said in response, I said to him in the form of a command: "The Immaculate Virgin was praised for three virtues. You must now tell me the fourth virtue that makes you so afraid of her." He immediately responded to me: "She is the only creature that can conquer me internally, because she has never been grazed by the smallest shadow of sin." If the demon speaks in this way of Mary, what must the exorcists say of Mary? In our experience, she is truly the mediatrix of all graces, because she is always the one who obtains the liberation of the demon. When one begins to exorcise a demoniac, the demon feels insulted and mocked; then the demon says to us: "I am fine here; I shall never leave from here; you cannot do anything against me; you are too weak; and you are wasting time." Gradually, however, Mary enters the scene, and then things change. The demon begins to say: "It is she who wishes it, against her I can do nothing. Tell her to stop; make her stop interceding for this person; she loves this creature too much. I am finished!"

It has often happened during exorcisms that I am suddenly faced with Mary's intervention; even at my first exorcism, the demon said to me: "I was so well here, but it is that one there who wished it; if it were not for her intervention, I would not ever have met you." St. Benedict concludes his famous "Discourse of the Aqueduct," a strictly theological theme, with a clear-cut phrase: "Mary is all the reason for my hope." I learned this phrase while, as a boy, I was waiting in front of the door of cell number 5 [over which the phrase was written] at San Giovanni Rotondo: it was Padre Pio's cell. At the time, I wished to study the context of this expression, which, at first glance, could seem simply devotional. But I was then able to taste the depth, the truth, and the connection between the doctrine and practical experience. Therefore, I willingly repeat to whoever is in a state of dejection or desperation, a frequent occurrence for those who are struck by evil spells: "Mary is all the reason for my hope."

Appendices

Appendix A

Maria Rita Viaggi Interviews Father Amorth

Christ's Power over the Devil

In the first of your books, An Exorcist Tells His Story, *you assert that the role of each creature depends on a Christ-centered formation. What does "Christ-centered formation" mean?*

Allow me to reference the prologue of the Gospel of St. John and the two Christological hymns of St. Paul—one the Letter to the Ephesians and the other the Letter to the Colossians—that begin, "everything was created by God through Christ and all things were created through Him and for Him, and in Him all things hold together" (see Col. 1:15–20). Therefore, Jesus Christ is the center: the pivot, the hinge, and the reason for being of each creature. I wished to begin with this. We must always begin from the center of creation, from the goal of creation, which is Jesus Christ, and then we must understand, in the light of Christ, the role of all created beings, in particular the intelligent beings, angels and men; and then the stars, the animal kingdom, and the vegetable kingdom. Everything holds together by a unique plan that has its reason for being in Jesus Christ.

Let us speak first and foremost of Christ's influence on the angels and demons.

Christ's influence is fundamental, but it is not emphasized very often. Everything begins from the idea that God, who created only good and beautiful things, created first the angels, spiritual beings that He endowed with intelligence and liberty; then He tested them. Some of these angels rebelled against God and became demons; the others remained faithful, and these are the angels. Then, according to common belief, God created man, also an intelligent being and also free, but composed of soul and body, not a pure spirit. Then God subjected man to a test, which he failed through the sin of Adam and Eve. Then the idea came to the mind of God to save man by means of Jesus Christ, by sending Him as the Savior. This approach does not take into account what we said before, that Christ is already the center of the universe and that everything was created through Him and by means of Him, and for which Christ is the center. The fact that Jesus was incarnated and came into the world as Savior and Victor, as He will come at the end of time, is the consequence of original sin, but independent of and apart from original sin everything was created by means of Christ. This is why the angels were also created in the sight of Christ and through Christ, and Christ gave the angels something that some of the early fathers express like this: "The angels would not have enjoyed the beatific vision of God if it had not been for the redemptive death of Christ through which they, in a fundamental manner, also experienced the redemption worked by God."

The Redemption of Christ has, then, cut off the power of Satan; but in all this, what is the role of Mary?

The power of Satan has been broken off by Christ. St. John is very explicit when he tells us that Christ, as the Incarnate Son of God, came to destroy the powers of the devil; then he tells us the salvific goal of Christ.

As for the role of Mary, here also we must begin from the beginning. If, in God's plan, everything was created in view of Christ as the center of the universe, there already was the Incarnate Word, but only as Victor, not as Savior, because first He had to suffer. Then after the Incarnation of the Word, the second creature thought of by God could not be other than the one in whom the Word of God, the second Person of the Most Holy Trinity, would be incarnated. Since, after the sin of Adam, Christ acquired the role of Savior and Redeemer, Mary also became associated in this role: above all by being exempt from original sin, as seen through the merits of Christ, because Mary is also a human creature, and she also would have been subjected to original sin if she had not been preventively exempt in view of the redemption by Christ. Already from the beginning of humanity, Mary was seen as more than the Mother of the Redeemer: God verifies this in the first pages of Genesis, in His forewarning and condemnation of Satan, the serpent: "I will put enmity between you and the woman, and between your seed and her seed; he shall bruise your head" (Gen. 3:15). Her seed is her Son, who is Christ. Mary is associated in this crushing of the demon's head in many great works of art.

Then the Evil One is a certainty. Thus, it is impossible to understand the redemptive work of Christ without taking into account the disruptive work of the Evil One — Satan, Lucifer, the devil. But who is he?

He is an angel created good that rebelled against God, distanced himself from God, and keeps trying to distance creatures from God. He is a bad angel that built hell by himself; indeed, God did not create hell; it was not in His original plans. Satan tried to find and drag as many men as he could to follow in his footsteps, go to the same place, and suffer the same punishment. In a certain sense, the devil became the anti-God, the one who combats the plans of God, because first he rebelled against God and against the plans that God had for him; and then he tried to get the rest of creation to rebel against God. This is the devil's strength, temptation, what we call the ordinary action of the devil, to which we are all subjected to such a point that even Jesus Christ, who became a true man like us, similar to us in all things except sin, allowed Himself to be tempted by Satan in the same way.

St. John says: "The whole world is in the power of the Evil One" (1 John 5:19). St. Paul says: "Ours is not a struggle against creatures made of flesh and blood but against the evil spirits of the dark world" (see Eph. 6:12). But, in effect, what power do these spirits have?

Undoubtedly it is a great power, because St. John tells us that all the world lies under the power of the Evil One; Jesus twice calls Satan, the Evil One, the "prince of this world"; and in the Second Letter to the Corinthians, St. Paul calls him the "god of this world," meaning that he has a great power in the world, a power that he exercises on each one of us.

Let us consider the three temptations of Christ. The devil is tremendously monotonous, and when I interrogated him on this point, he said to me that even if he is monotonous, we men fall for it just the same; when, for example, in the third temptation, he offers the man Jesus all the kingdoms of the earth, saying: "Look, I shall show you all the kingdoms of the earth, they are mine and I shall give them to you if you bow down and adore me," Jesus did not say to him that he is a liar and that all the kingdoms of the earth belong to the Father. Rather, Jesus responded to him with a phrase from Sacred Scripture: "It is written that you shall adore God alone" (see Matt. 4:8–10). Jesus meant that the devil can also make some of these human promises to men and they can fall for them, since they prostrate themselves to Satan out of ambition and out of love of power; but these human, earthly goods are given to man so that he can make good use of them for the advantage of his brothers and sisters.

We have spoken of Satan, then of Lucifer, then the devil, but is there a difference, or are they references to the same spirit? Is it possible that the devil can present himself under the form of a person?

The number of demons is incalculable, and as with the hierarchy of angels there is also a hierarchy of demons. We know, for example, that the leader for the angels is St. Michael the Archangel, and for the demons we know that the leader is presented under various names, which I think are synonyms; for example, Satan, Beelzebul, and Lucifer. This last one is not strictly a biblical name; according to our exorcistical experience, it is a different devil from Satan, but some would also consider it a synonym of Satan. We also know that the demons are numerous and that the Bible presents them under various names that are hierarchically dependent. They have a strict internal hierarchy like that in criminal organizations, all of which yield power through fear and oppression, not love, as with the angels.

What powers do demons have?

All demons are engaged in tempting men to do evil in order to detach them from God and to try to destroy God's plan.

The Devil Exists

At this point, is it necessary to make a clarification. We have reached our first certainty, that the devil exists and that, if we deny it, we would be denying the sacrifice of Christ. Correct?

It would also be a misunderstanding of the plan of creation. Not understanding the devil would not mean misunderstanding God; rather, it would mean misunderstanding the plan of redemption, which is everything that happened following the sin of Adam, original sin. Consequently, for man, salvation became an indispensable necessity because man could not save himself.

I would also like to add that human reason has only a vague perception of these realities; how, then, can human reason reach belief in the existence of God, from creation to Creator? In the history of humanity, even the peoples before the Jews had a sense that there were spirits of good and spirits of evil; it is only through revelation, however, that we have the certainty and clarity regarding all these insensible, invisible realities. It is only from revelation that we know with certainty God, the immortality of the soul, the existence of the angels and the demons, and the existence of paradise and hell; although, even in the most primitive religions, man also arrived at some vague awareness of these realities.

We have mentioned that Satan and the angels are pure spirits; they do not have a body. Therefore, in order to present themselves in a way to be perceived by man, they must assume a false form, adapted to the human level; and they assume it according to the mission they wish to fulfill. We see, for example, that the Archangel Raphael, in order to accompany Tobias on a trip, has to make himself noticeably present; therefore, he assumes the form of a youth, a human body.

Does the devil exist with horns, a tail, and the wings of a bat, or with the head of a billy goat and hoofs? I would say that these forms are intended to represent decadence. They are characteristics of a man who is becoming more comfortable with the animal kingdom [than with the human]; a man who has horns, a tail and wings is a man who has some animalistic elements that demonstrate his fallen state. In reality, we cannot represent the devil, so it is he who presents himself in a temporary, false form that suits his intentions. For example, if he wishes to frighten, he assumes the form of a monster or of something that generates terror; if he wishes to seduce, he can assume the form of a seductive young girl, as it happened to Padre Pio when the devil vexed him at Venafro (Molise). There are also some famous stories about the struggles in the desert between St. Anthony and the devil.

Thus, the demon, in order to make himself perceptible to the senses, assumes a temporary, false form because, as a pure spirit, he has no body and is not perceptible to man; thus, he assumes a form suitable to his proposed objectives.

St. Augustine says: "If God gave Satan a free hand, none of us would remain alive." He cannot do whatever he wants, but he can cause us many problems. Can we speak of the ordinary and of the extraordinary activities? What does this mean?

It means that God is the Creator, it is He who holds life; and the demon, being anti-God, is the destroyer. God is the one who wishes good and happiness; the demon is the one who wishes evil and unhappiness, and he succeeds very well in his task—I add, however, only on the condition that man agrees to it, that man opens the door to him. As a rule, the demon cannot do anything without human consent. We learned that from the beginning, from the Fall of Adam and Eve, who, having been born with intelligence and free will, were able and should have obeyed God but chose instead deliberately to disobey God and to obey the suggestions of the devil; they could have and should have acted differently. Therefore, the devil has some great powers if we give in to him. The devil is anti-God; anti-God the Creator; the destroyer. Thus, we have the phrase from St. Augustine: "If he could, he would kill all of us." Not being able to kill or to destroy, he tries to draw us to his side. He does all of this through his ordinary action, temptation.

There is also the extraordinary action of the devil. The devil can give a series of disturbances that in most cases are possible only with human consent. The devil gives these disturbances in exchange for the gifts that he offers to those who give themselves to him. For example, gifts of foresight, riches, success, and power are always accompanied by the greatest sufferings, because the demon can do only evil. Therefore, he treats his adorers very badly. The figure of Faust, who, to gain happiness on this earth, gives his soul to the devil because the afterlife does not matter to him, is a poetic figure that is completely unreal; those who give themselves to the devil receive worldly gifts and advantages that are always tied to terrible sufferings.

We have touched on clairvoyance and foreknowledge. Are these phenomena always managed by the demon?

They are not. Some of these phenomena are part of the makeup of natural phenomena, studied particularly by parapsychology as they relate to the paranormal; that is, what science studies but does not yet accept, because the studies in this field are in part either behind or impossible. Let us recall what Hamlet says: "There are so many things under the sun that are not written in the philosophies." Therefore, we find ourselves in a world that has an immense richness, and we arrive at knowing it only up to a certain point.

Let us return to what you speak of so well in your book: the six disturbances: possession, vexation, obsession, infestation, physical disturbances, and dependency, and their four causes.
Yes, I have a list, but it is not agreed upon by everyone. I tried hard to create some terms that would be shared and used to build a common language, which does not yet exist; so I listed six types of diabolical disturbances that the demon can give, and the ways one can avoid them or be cured if one runs up against them.

We can take them individually and say something about each one; let's begin with the disturbances: possession, obsession, vexation, and infestation.

Possession is the devil's most serious disturbance, in which one nearly has the impression that the demon is inside a person, taking possession of him to the point that he speaks from the person's mouth and commands the rest of his body. These extraordinary phenomena can occur nearly theatrically if we consider the Gospel example of the demoniac of Gerasa, whose demon has a superhuman form, the capacity to speak many languages, and knowledge of hidden things (Mark 5:1ff.). Because of the knowledge of hidden things, many are afraid of assisting at my exorcisms; they have the idea that the demon will tell their sins; to be truthful, this has never happened to me, but the demon does know things that are hidden.

Possession, as I have mentioned, is the strongest form, but it does not always have obvious characteristics, such as a man rolling around on the floor or someone who received blessed water feeling as if he is on fire. There are many forms of diabolical possession, and the more common forms are not sensational demonstrations of phenomena; they are solely great sufferings, great physical and psychic disturbances. At times during the exorcism, demons, even at the moment they are forced to reveal themselves, are able to refrain from showing flashy external forms.

One experiences vexation when the demon causes a person serious disturbances but not possession. It is not easy to distinguish vexation from natural evils. In the Bible, for example—and for me, biblical examples are always the clearest and most emblematic—Job was struck in his affections with the sudden death of all his ten children; in his possessions, by suddenly going from extremely rich to extremely poor; and in his health, from being heathy to being covered with sores from his head to his feet. But he was not a demoniac; there was no presence of the demon in him, and I know so many persons like this. We can say that the most serious cases of possession remain numerically limited even today, but like all the evil disturbances, they are increasing; in contrast, the cases of vexations are numerous.

A great many people are struck in their relationships; therefore, they cannot find a husband or a wife, or a marriage or an engagement falls apart without any obvious motive. Others are struck in their personal goods and property; for example, entrepeneurs who all at once commit some enormous errors and are reduced to misery or without motive find themselves on the pavement. I have known so many cases of merchants with shops doing extremely well, then all of a sudden no one sets foot in the place. Then there are so many persons who are struck with physical disturbances. We also note that all these things could depend on natural motives as well as evil; therefore, it is important to know how to distinguish, from certain signs, whether these disturbances have an evil development or a development that is natural. Some see them as nearly synonymous, but I tend to make distinctions.

Obsession is when one is assailed by obsessive, unconquerable thoughts that he absolutely cannot dismiss; and because he cannot liberate himself from them, they bring him ever closer to desperation and even suicide. One of the successes the demon aims for, as a destroyer, is to bring the person to this point of desperation and then suicide, and unfortunately, sometimes he succeeds, above all in cases of obsession. It is the unconquerable obsessive thoughts that bring the person to desperation and then to the desire to attempt or to commit suicide.

Infestation is a term that I reserve solely for disturbances on houses, objects, and animals. From Patristic times, Origen gives us examples of exorcisms performed not only to liberate man but also places, objects, and animals.

The Gospel presents us with the demoniac of Gerasa, in which the demons ask the Lord to permit them to go into a herd of pigs and at the moment they entered these animals, they became demoniac. As for exorcisms on places, I would say that the most common reason exorcists are called to exorcise houses are the strange phenomena and noises heard in these places that cannot be humanly explained.

According to the list, among the physical disturbances, there is dependency.

Physical disturbances are disturbances to the body that the demon gives to certain holy persons and that the Lord permits for their sanctification. Let us take, for example, the Curé d'Ars, who was often beaten and thrown down from the bed. Padre Pio also had this experience; once he even needed stitches along his eyebrow, because the demon, after throwing him down from his bed, beat his head against the floor. These are physical pains, but there is no presence of the demon in their person, and they are not like vexations, external sufferings that strike material goods, affections, or health; rather, these disturbances are immediate physical illnesses caused by the demon and permitted by the Lord for the sanctification of the person.

I believe that among these examples we should include the disturbance that St. Paul speaks of in a terse manner, when he tells us that in order to keep him humble, the Lord has permitted, nearly like a thorn in the flesh, an angel of Satan, therefore a demon, to beat him. He begged Him to have this taken from him, obviously physical and of diabolical origin, but instead it followed him to the end of his life, even to the tomb (2 Cor. 12:7ff.).

We arrive at the causes; how do we end up with all of this? Is it from patronizing dangerous places and people, or from being in a state of sin?

I make out four motives for which one can fall into these six forms of evil disturbances.

I add as the sixth disturbance the demonic dependence that one acquires doing the so-called blood pact with Satan; when one voluntarily places himself, willingly and knowingly, and with total adhesion, to dependency on Satan and thus becomes a slave of Satan, solely to obtain some favors and human successes.

How does one get into this situation? It is important to be aware of the causes, because knowing the causes is the best prevention and resolution.

The first cause is the permission of God—that is, when there is no human intervention. This is substantiated in the Bible with the case of Job, where it is the devil who procures these disturbances. This is also the case of St. Paul;[17] the Lord permits them; we also find this cause in the lives of saints who had a diabolical possession.

In 1988, the Holy Father, John Paul II, beatified the little Arabic nun Sister Maria of the Crucified Jesus, born a few kilometers from Nazareth, who presently is the only person entered into the album of the blessed and the saints who has had some moments in which the demon possessed her in a total manner, to such a degree that she needed to be exorcised. Also here, the evil was permitted, with the objective of sanctifying her and making her practice patience and endurance. The Lord permitted these sufferings in reparation for the sins of humanity.

This, then, is the first cause, in which there is no human intervention.

What Evil Spells Are

An evil spell, or simply a spell, is one of the causes of demonic actions. A person can run into one of those six evils of the extraordinary actions of the devil that we have just defined because he has been subjected to an evil spell. The spell is defined like this: "To do evil to a person through the work of the devil." There are many ways an evil spell can be done, the most common are: tying or binding, cursing, the evil eye, macumba, and voodoo.

In this situation, we have an oddity. The person who is struck is faultless; it is not the recipient who made an agreement with a

---

[17] "And to keep me from being too elated by the abundance of revelations, a thorn was given me in the flesh, a messenger of Satan, to harass me, to keep me from being too elated. Three times I besought the Lord about this, that it should leave me; but he said to me, 'My grace is sufficient for you, for my power is made perfect in weakness'" (2 Cor. 12:7–8).

demon. Rather, the agreement with the demon to open the door to Satan is made through the will of another person, the one who requested this spell. It must be noted, however, that very often the evil spells do not reach their targeted objective, and this can happen when an evil spell is done against a person who lives in the grace of God and, being united to the Lord, is shielded.

This says it well that if we observe the commandments and receive the sacraments regularly, we are nearly immune.

I say nearly immune to evil spells because, as we have mentioned, the Lord permits certain persons to submit to demonic evils for their sanctification. This, as I mentioned above, is the first cause of evil spells. But as a general rule, we can say that a person who lives in the state of grace is nearly immune from evil spells.

I would like to emphasize here those great words of Paul VI when, in his famous discourse on the devil of November 15, 1972, he offered a question: "How can we defend ourselves from these evils that the devil inflicts on us?" Responding directly, he said: "All that defends us from sin defends us from the Evil One." Therefore, to live in the grace of God, through prayer and the sacraments, protects us from attacks that come from or could be provoked by others through evil spells.

Therefore, the Evil One exists and has some powers that undermine us. How do we defend ourselves? Through an exorcism?

Let us say immediately that the greatest defense against an evil disturbance is the prayer of liberation; I begin immediately from here, not from the exorcism. The exorcism is a sacramental instituted by the Church; it is reserved for bishops and priests appointed by the bishops, and it excludes all those braggarts, wizards, and the like who sell themselves as exorcists but who cannot do exorcisms.

The exorcism is a sacramental; therefore, it is a sacred ritual that can be administered exclusively either by a bishop or by a priest who has been appointed expressly for this purpose by the bishop, not by a layperson.

Because exorcism is a sacramental, a ritual instituted by the Church, the Church can also change these rules; the Church could even grant laymen the authority to practice the exorcistate—that is, to become exorcists.

Ecclesiastical discipline has changed throughout the times, and it can still change. For example, in the first three centuries, all Christians did exorcisms without need of any permission; then the exorcistate was instituted in order to avoid having persons fall into the clutches of knaves and tricksters who began to spring up. Thus, the Church of the Latin or Roman rite instituted the sacramental of exorcism in order to guarantee the qualifications of those who administered this type of exorcism. Unlike the Latin Church, the Eastern Church always considered exorcism, even up to the present, a personal charism given to bishops, priests, and laity according to the ways of the Holy Spirit.

Exorcism is stronger than a prayer of liberation, which everyone can do. Jesus was very clear: "Those who believe in me will cast out demons in my name." These, however, are not exorcisms; even if the goal is identical, they are prayers of liberation—that is, they are private prayers that anyone who believes in Jesus Christ, even a child, can utilize in His name in order to chase demons. The exorcism, however, is more than a prayer of liberation; it is a sacramental that involves the authority of the Church, and it can be administered only by a bishop or by a priest and therefore has more strength per se and more efficacy than the simple private prayer.

How far back do exorcisms go?

We can place exorcisms in the fourth century. We cannot define an exact date, but the insertion of the minor order of exorcistate falls in the fourth century among the orders entrusted to bishops.

How is an exorcism carried out? How long does it last? I know that there are two Rituals, but which one is current? Is there an interim Ritual, which is the Roman Ritual, and a new experimental Ritual? One includes twenty norms, the other five, if I am not mistaken?

The entire Roman Ritual, which includes the administration of the sacraments, has been reformed. Also, after the council, the administration of baptism and marriage was updated according to the norms of the council and the customs and practices of our times. Let us also consider the great passage from celebrating the liturgy in Latin to the vernacular, in particular the Mass. The only part of the Ritual that has not been reformed and is still currently completely operative is the Ritual of Exorcism. There is, at the same time, a reform in progress.

In your book, Father Amorth, you say that exorcisms can have a diagnostic effect. What are the symptoms that determine one or the other?

I maintain that it is only through the exorcism that we are able to know with certainty if an illness is an evil spell or not, if there is the presence of the demon in a person, or if a person is possessed. All the symptoms could also be explained naturally, and in cases of natural illnesses, an exorcism is necessary to provide certainty.

Do you use traps?

All exorcists use some traps because the demon does everything in order to hide himself; therefore, because he does not manifest his presence, we think up some traps that will allow the demon, if he is there, to show himself.

Then the demon is not obvious in the first session?

No, at times, it takes much time to know this; however, there is the opposite danger of seeing the demon where he is not. In the majority of cases, the persons who turn to us present us with a symptom that is too insignificant for a demonic presence. For example, they bring me a person whom they tell me is a demoniac or who has a demonic illness because the medical doctors were not able to cure him or the medications are ineffective; or they are not even able to do a diagnosis. All of that alone is not enough to say there is a demonic presence.

Another symptom, the most common, is aversion to the sacred, which is revealed by minor symptoms, such as yawning or falling asleep during the liturgy, or greater symptoms, such as when one rebels when entering a church and is forced to go away in order not to commit foolish actions and become violent. Other more serious symptoms are when a person feels that the blessed water used on him is fire. But even in this case, it could be solely a suggestion, and this solitary reaction may not be sufficient; for example, there are some people who are sensitive to water, and when drinking it, they question whether it is blessed or not; so this also could depend on natural motives.

There are some symptoms that I call symptoms of suspicion, which, taken individually, are not sufficient to say that there is an evil presence; for example, when the person says that his illnesses are physical or psychic or that he suffers from the impossibility to study or work, and that they began when he took part in séances, or when, out of curiosity, he attended a satanic sect, or when he began practices of occultism. Initially, this also is reason for suspicion, but by itself it is not enough. Each symptom by itself is not enough. Put together, however, some of these symptoms are sufficient for the exorcist to proceed to the exorcism or beforehand, to organize prayers of liberation. We advise always to do the prayers of liberation first, and if one sees that during the course of a series of prayers of liberation, it is not enough, and that these symptoms become ever stronger, violent and conspicuous, then it means that it is worth proceeding to the exorcism.

What are the requirements for administering an exorcism?

It is curious, but I must say that we exorcize more women than men and more young people than older people. I have not found any motives for this, but there can be many reasons. A woman, more than a man, is exposed to certain curiosities such as going to fortune-tellers or wizards and participating in séances, and therefore, they are exposed to more risk. This is also true with young people. I think of how the young people today travel; when I was going on vacation, I was content to go to the hills around my city. Today the young people content themselves going to Algeria, India, or Papuasia, often in order to attend the school of a guru. But then there is no need to go to India to find a guru; today gurus are all around us. Those who seek us exorcists have usually associated with dangerous persons or places out of curiosity or stupidity, or because they are influenced by friends.

At times, it happens that a person has disturbances that are either physical or work related, and everything is going to ruin; so he takes the medical route, but to no avail. I knew and exorcised a seventeen-year-old girl who had already visited the principal clinics of Europe, and being young, acquired a complete distrust in official medicine in general and in psychiatry in particular.

Generally, a person seeks medical help first and then, at times [perhaps as a last resort], will try the ways of magic, seeking out wizards and fortune-tellers.

I would like to stop here for a moment on this point because people do not know the danger they can procure with an evil intervention of an "unauthorized person," such as a wizard or a witch, who, rather than help, can even double the effect of the evil spell, whatever it was.

Even worse, one could increase the negative effect a hundred-fold or, as it happens, create a presence that was not initially there, because the vast majority of wizards, I would say 99.99 percent, are tricksters who have nothing other than the power of suggestion. It must be noted, however, that the power of suggestion can create some psychic illnesses, because one can do evil with a suggestion. One can also say that a suggestion can do good, because, if one has an evil caused by suggestion, it is possible that a contrary suggestion makes the person feel better. This does not change the fact that most wizards are tricksters and self-proclaiming benefactors who advertise through the mass media, playing the part of the lion. The majority of these persons deceive their neighbor. I must add that there are also wizards who are connected to Satan that are true and proper sorcerers.

It is interesting that you speak of the exorcist dealing with the presence of the wizard in the person who turned to him rather than with the evil spell or with the devil, with whom he will deal later on.

It is interesting, but [not accurate;] therefore, it is necessary to clarify things: the wizard, who is still a living human being, cannot be present in the person, and even if he were no longer in existence, it would have no relevance, because only his influence is present in this person. One may have the impression that one is speaking with the wizard, but the wizard is not present; no person, living or dead, can be present inside another person. Regarding this, I wish to say that immediately after death, we go either to paradise or to hell or to purgatory. Two Church councils, the Council of Lyons and the Council of Florence, have defined this reality; therefore, when I hear reports of wandering souls or souls in pain because they are in the afterlife and do not yet know which path to take, I say that they are all stories.

Then we do not recognize the Tibetan Book of the Dead?[18]

No, we do not recognize it, and we will never recognize it; in fact, there is no proof. When one goes in depth in certain cases, one sees that they are cases of suggestion. Allow me to make a clarification: it is necessary that the person be truly dead in order to go to paradise or to hell or to purgatory; at times one can be in a state of a deep coma, which seems like an apparent death and can last a long time. In these cases, it is not easy to establish the exact instant of death; it is not enough to see that a person no longer moves and breathes to say that he is dead. It requires a doctor to certify a death, and we have known cases in which the medical doctors themselves are so uncertain that they postpone the burial of a person until they feel secure enough to decide.

---

[18] The Tibetan *Book of the Dead* is a Buddhist text written by a Tibetan monk that describes death from the Tibetan point of view, which are the experiences consciousness has after death in the interval between death and the next rebirth.

Anyway, when there is death, the soul goes immediately to paradise or to hell or to purgatory.

Therefore, it is impossible for a living person to be present in another living person, and the soul immediately finds its place. What activities does the soul have in the afterlife?
There are some certainties and some obscurities on this topic. St. Thomas says that we know little of the souls in the afterlife; therefore, we must take into account some of the private experiences of the saints, persons united to God and living a holy life, not that of delirious and confused persons.

We know from the dogma of the Communion of Saints that the souls in paradise can receive our prayers and intercede for us. We know that the souls in purgatory can also receive our intercessory prayers and, in turn, can intercede for us. We must note that this is a rapport through God, never a direct rapport between a soul and us. Only in extraordinary cases does God permit the soul of a deceased to present himself to a human being. That, however, would be an extraordinary case, wished for and permitted by God, not dependent on human stratagems. But I refute all those theories, all those forms of spiritism and all those movements, such as the belief that one can evoke the dead to speak with them, because this is impossible. Only God can take the initiative; it cannot be done solely with human means. This is also the case with automatic writing, psychophonia, and other claims of contact with the deceased.[19] The normal contact

---

[19] Automatic writing or psychology is an alleged psychic ability that allows a person to produce written words without consciously writing. The words are claimed to arise from a subconscious, spiritual, or supernatural source. Psychophonia is

is never direct but is always through God, as with their receiving our prayers of suffrage and interceding for us. Even in the parable of the rich man, Dives, and Lazarus, it is interesting to note that when Dives finds himself in hell, he does not ever speak directly with Lazarus, who is in paradise; rather, he speaks to Abraham and asks him to send Lazarus.

During an exorcism, can an exorcist interact with these souls?

This topic is a bit debatable and requires some study, but in general, the response is no. A theological investigation of the biblical texts would be helpful; very often they contain some implicit truths, and on this topic, explicit truths do not exist. At times, in fact, when theologians are thoroughly analyzing the biblical texts, they discover some truths that are implicitly contained. For example, that Our Lady was assumed into heaven is a truth that finds its foundation in the Bible, but not explicitly.

We would like theologians to make a study of which activities are possible for the souls of the deceased in the period that we call the intermediary period—that is, between their death and their definitive location, and what their definitive state will be at the resurrection of the body at the end of the world. There is only this life, and each one decides his eternal future in this life; that never changes; for the soul the situation after death is a temporary situation, however, because the soul is waiting for the body.

I would like theologians to analyze thoroughly which activities are possible for souls in the intermediary period, particularly if

---

the name given by Spiritism (founder Allan Kardec, author of *The Medium's Book*) and some other spiritualist traditions to the speaking of spirits through a medium.

it is possible for the demon to make use of a condemned soul in order to torment a person, or even to have the soul torment the person directly. For now, as a rule, we exorcists support the norm provided in the Roman Ritual (no. 14) that states, if the demon tries to camouflage himself to appear as the soul of a deceased or a saint, do not believe it, because it is a devil's trick.

I know that in the afterlife there is no time, but in what does the intermediary period of which you have spoken to us consist?
It is the time that passes between the actual moment of death and the moment of the Parousia, which is the triumphal coming of Christ and the resurrection of the dead that completes the happiness of man. Even the happiness of St. Francis of Assisi in paradise is an incomplete happiness, because his body is not yet participating in it and man is made of both body and soul. So even today, we must turn to St. Thomas for a deeper understanding of these themes because they have been neglected. He tells us that one of the most difficult realities to demonstrate rationally is how the human soul can live and be happy without the body; it is one of those realities that we know solely by faith.

Let us take a moment to clarify what we said previously: as soon as the body dies, the soul immediately finds a place; but now we are saying that there is an intermediary period; what does this mean? Is it a reference solely to the Parousia?
Let us also say that for the one who immediately has his incomplete definitive placement in paradise or is already in hell; purgatory is a transitory state that we could call pre-paradise. From this point of view, the placement is definitive. What is not yet definitive is the personality of the individual, because he is not soul and body, but only soul, for which in this definitive

placement, either the torment [in purgatory or hell] or the happiness [in heaven] is still incomplete, since it lacks the participation of the body.

Can a person who assists at an exorcism remain in some way contaminated?

The exorcism is not contagious, nor are the evils caused by the demon contagious. One possessed by the demon is not someone infected [with a germ or a virus]. I know many families in which a spouse has a diabolical possession and is being exorcised, but the other spouse has no damage and has no need for an exorcism, and neither do the children. Therefore, diabolical possession is not contagious, and there is no need to fear acquiring any damage during an exorcism or during the prayers of liberation.

Appendix B

Prayers of Liberation Used by Father Amorth

The Sacraments Are the Most Efficacious

Father Amorth writes:

Often I am asked to suggest prayers of liberation from the devil or from evil influences, illnesses, and sufferings that are accessible to everyone—priests and laity—without need of any authorization.

First, I wish to say that the sacraments and the word of God are more efficacious than our personal invocations. When we turn to the Lord, the most significant requirement, and it is affirmed often in the Gospel, is faith. My experience has taught me that to receive the liberating presence of the Lord effectively, the following sequential steps must be observed:

1. Confession, which is the sacrament directly focused on snatching souls from Satan; it implies a heartfelt pardon: "Forgive us our trespasses as we ..."
2. Holy Mass
3. Communion
4. Eucharistic adoration
5. Biblical and liturgical prayer: the psalms and the canticles of the Bible; the Creed, the Gloria, and so forth
6. The Rosary and other traditional prayers

Only in light of these general concepts are the following prayers efficacious. Their valuation and collocation do not depend on an automatic or magical result; rather, they depend on the faith of the one who humbly turns to the Father, the Virgin Mary, the angels, and the saints.

In the presence of illnesses and spells, it is a good thing to double down on one's spiritual practices and prayers; in particular: to the Holy Spirit, the names of Jesus and Mary, and the Most Holy One. Regarding the Virgin Mary, her role is not secondary. Mary is not only the Mother of the Redeemer; she is also the collaborator in His redemptive work; it is not by chance that painters and sculptors represent her in the act of crushing the head of the devil. She is a powerful intercessor.

Pray to the Angels and the Archangels

Further on in the celestial order, the angels and archangels are valid intercessors in the struggle against the Evil One; for example, the book of Revelation relates the war in heaven between the good angels, led by Michael, the head of the heavenly militia, and the rebel angels, led by Satan; the Archangel prevails, and the enemies are thrown into hell:

> Now war arose in heaven, Michael and his angels fighting against the dragon; and the dragon and his angels fought, but they were defeated and there was no longer any place for them in heaven. And the great dragon was thrown down, that ancient serpent, who is called the devil and Satan, the deceiver of the whole world—he was thrown down to the earth, and his angels were thrown down with him. (12:7–9)

Therefore, one usually invokes Michael the Archangel as the head of the angelic hosts; I also invoke all the guardian angels of all those present, among whom, obviously, is St. Gabriel the Archangel, who is my patron.

Pray to the Saints

Among the other saints, one often hears of St. Benedict as "the patron of exorcists"; in reality, it has not been historically proven that Pope Honorius III named him such. Since an official patron of exorcists does not exist, however, we invoke him because he demonstrated great strength against the devil, given that he often drove him away. Benedict's medal also has a notable effect against the Evil One.

Each exorcist invokes the saint to whom he is personally devoted or to whom the exorcistate is devoted. There is no saint who has a particular power against the devil; all the saints have some power. Moreover, there are many cases of saints who have been tormented by the devil. Among the most emblematic, because it concerns a fairly recent business, is the Carmelite nun known as "the Little Arab": Sister Maria of the Crucified Jesus. In the course of her life, she was often subjected to diabolic possession and needed to be exorcised to obtain liberation. On the other side, we know various cases of saints, among whom are St. John Bosco, the Curé d'Ars, Padre Pio, St. Gemma Galgani, St. Angela de Foligno, Father Calabria—one could continue to cite saints forever—who had diabolic vexations from which they were liberated, thanks solely to prayer and the reception of the sacraments.

Fear Sin, not the Devil

The Bible never tells us to fear the devil; it assures us that we can and must resist him strongly in our faith. The Bible tells us that we must fear sin; and because all saints combat sin, therefore,

THE DEVIL IS AFRAID OF ME

all saints combat the devil. Paul VI affirmed it in his discourse on the devil: "Everything that defends us from sin defends us from Satan."

We must only fear not being in the state of grace with God, and this means that we must confess our sins, participate at holy Mass, receive the Eucharist, spend time in Eucharistic adoration, and pray, especially the psalms and the Rosary; all these, among others, are the best remedies against the extraordinary activity of the devil; we are shielded if we remain in the grace of God. The great saint John Chrysostom says that the devil, in spite of himself, is a sanctifier of souls, because he is defeated and because the suffering he procures in these holy people, when offered to the Lord, are a means of sanctification.

Father Stanzione's Reminder about the Following Prayers

Father Amorth emphasizes that no one should use prayers to perform exorcisms on their relatives, friends, or persons close to them. The prayers of liberation that are included in this book must be utilized as personal prayers of self-liberation: reciting them does not mean that you are performing an exorcism; that is something that is solely the purview of the priests who are granted special authority from their bishops and, as such, represent the authority of the Church.

Apart from the prayers presented here, prayers that should not be forgotten are the psalms, particularly those that specifically ask for liberation from the enemy: 3, 10, 12, 21, 30, 34, 67, 90; the recitation of the Liturgy of the Hours; and the Rosary.

The more we turn to grace, the more the infernal enemy, already defeated by Christ, is also defeated by us who are united mystically to the Liberator. Appendix 2 of the new Ritual of exorcism offers a series of supplications and prayers that the faithful, individually or in a group, can adopt when they are attacked by the demon. Those prayers are not composed for others; they are intended for the faithful when praying for themselves. One presumes that the attacks are of the ordinary action of Satan and that there is no need of a liberating intervention or exorcism, that is, of someone who prays for others. In such a case, one would seek an exorcist priest who would perform the exorcism.

Besides praying specific prayers, it is necessary to intensify one's spiritual life, through the ordinary means (the sacraments) and through additional prayers with specific intentions.

The following prayers are appropriate for all Christians to recite for themselves and for others.

Prayer for Liberation from the Devil
(Poema Historica, de se ipso; PG 37, 1280)

Deliver me, deliver me, O immortal God, from the foreign
　　hand;
that I may not be tried by evil deeds
and that the pharaoh does not torment me.
Do not let me fall into the nets,
O Christ, of Your adversary;
that he may not lead me into the dark Babylon,
all covered with wounds.
Permit me to remain in Your vestibule
and to sing praises at Your feet.
Let not the fire of Sodom
fall like rain upon my head.
Protect me under Your powerful mantle;
distance from me all misfortune.
Woe to me, Christ, the dragon has returned.
Woe to me, he multiplies his fury.

Woe to me, I have tasted the tree of knowledge.
Woe to me, the jealous one has inspired me with
    thoughts of jealousy.
I have nothing divine, and I am chased from paradise.
O sword, mitigate a bit your burning flame.
Open again the Garden of Eden,
as the Crucified Christ did so for the thief. Amen.

Prayer over the Oil for the Sick[20]
We pray to You who possess every power, You who are the Savior
of all men, the Father of our Lord and Savior Jesus Christ; we
beseech You, from the heaven of Your only Son, pour out on
this oil Your healing power, so that those who will receive this
anointing or those who anoint Your creatures may destroy every
evil and every infirmity and every satanic power, distance every
impure spirit, chase away every evil spirit, eradicate every fever
and chill, debilitate every weakness, bring grace and the remis-
sion of sins, be the remedy of life and salvation, the health and
integrity of the soul, body, and mind and the fullness of strength.
May each diabolical enterprise, each satanic power, Lord, each
snare of the adversary, each torment, each pain, blow, clash or
evil shadow fear your Name that we invoke and fear the Name
of Your only Son; distance them from the soul and body of Your
servants, Lord, so that the One who, for us, was crucified and
resurrected, who took upon Himself our ills and our infirmities,
Jesus Christ, who will come to judge the living and the dead,
may receive glory and honor for ever and ever. Amen.

[20] A. Hamman, *Prayer of the First Christians* (Milan, 1962),
    179–180.

The First Baptismal Exorcism
(From the Orthodox Euchologion)[21]

The Lord has come into the world, has dwelled among men to break your tyranny, O Satan, and to liberate them. He triumphed on the Cross of your power when the sun was obscured and the earth trembled, when the tombs were opened and the bodies of the saints were raised up. In His death, he destroyed you, the one who had the power over death. I exorcise you in the name of God, who has shown the tree of life and who established the cherubim, the angels, with the sword of fire to protect it. Back, Satan! I exorcise you for the One who walks on the waves of the sea as well as on land and who commands the fury of the winds. I exorcise you for the One whose gaze dries up the abysses and whose threat causes the mountains to melt. It is still He who through us commands you. Remain in your fear, go out, get out of this creature, and do not come back here, do not meet her any-more, have no more influence on her, neither during the night or during the day, not in the morning or at noon; rather, return to your hell until the appointed day of the great judgment. God is enthroned upon the cherubim. He contemplates the abysses. In His presence the angels tremble: the thrones, the dominions, the principalities, the virtues, the powers, the cherubs with many eyes, and the seraphim with six wings.

Before Him, heaven and earth tremble, the sea and all that enclose it. Go out and abandon the soldier who is elected by

---

[21] The Euchologion is one of the chief liturgical books of the Orthodox Church and Eastern Catholic Churches, containing the portions of the services that are said by the bishop, priest, or deacon. There are several different volumes of the book in use.

Christ our God and is marked by his seal. It is in Him that I exorcise you, through the One who advances on the wings of the wind and who makes flames of fire His servants. Get out of this creature; abandon her, you and your power and your angels, so that the name of the Father, of the Son, and of the Holy Spirit may be glorified, now and forever and ever. Amen.

The Second Baptismal Exorcism
(From the Orthodox Euchologion)

Through the holy, terrible, and glorious God, for the One who is incomprehensible and inconceivable in all His works and in His power, for the One who has destined you to the anguish of eternal begging, O devil, and in the name of the Lord Jesus Christ, the true God, we His unworthy servants, command you and all the powers working with you. Through the power of Jesus Christ, who possesses all the power in heaven and on earth and who said to the deaf mute: "Come out of this man and return no more to him," I exorcise you, impure, foreign, and evil spirit. I recognize the weakness of your power; you do not even have power over swine. Remember the One who ordered you, according to your request, to enter the herd of pigs. Fear God: by His command, the earth is fixed on the waters. He created heaven; He set the mountains on their level and the plains to their measure. He put sand as the limit of the sea and created a firm path in the waters. He touches the mountains and they cover themselves with smoke. He dresses the light like a cloak; He extends the sky like a tent. He covers the peak of His dwelling with the waters. He establishes the earth on its firmament. He calls the water of the seas and spreads them over the face of the earth.

Go out of and abandon the one who is preparing for the holy illumination. I exorcise you through the redemptive Passion of our Lord Jesus Christ, His venerable Body and Blood and His terrible return — because He will come to judge all the earth. He will punish you in the fire of hell, you and your power, and He will toss you into the darkness, where the worms crawl incessantly and where the fire never goes out; because power is with Christ, our God, with the Father and with the Holy Spirit, now and forever, world without end. Amen.

The Third Baptismal Exorcism
(From the Orthodox Euchologion)

Lord of hosts, O God, who heals from every evil and from every sickness, look at Your servant and examine him, try him, distance from him each diabolical action. Punish the impure spirits and hunt them, purify the work of Your hands and through Your irresistible force, put Satan under Your feet and give him victory over the devil and the unclean spirits. May he be judged worthy of the heavenly and immortal mysteries after having received Your mercy and given You glory, Father, Son, and Holy Spirit, now and forever and ever. Amen.

The Fourth Baptismal Exorcism
(From the Orthodox Euchologion)

Lord and Master, You created man in Your image and likeness; You gave him power to reach eternal life, and afterward You did not despise him or scorn him when he fell into sin. Rather, You gave him salvation in the world through the Incarnation of your Son. You Yourself, after freeing Your creature from the slavery of the enemy, welcome him into Your heavenly kingdom, so that the light of Your gospel can shine on him; You join to his life an angel of light that liberates from all the evil of the enemy, from the encounter with the Evil One, from the noonday devil, and from perverse illusions. Cast out from him every evil and impure spirit that hides in his heart. Chase away from him the spirit of iniquity, the spirit of idolatry, the spirit of lies, boundless greed, and all impurity, all that is inspired by the devil's instigations. Make of him an intelligent sheep of Your Christ's holy flock, an honorable member of Your Church, a sanctified vessel, a child of light, and an heir of your kingdom, so that, after having lived according to your commandments, conserving intact your seal, and keeping his vestment immaculate, he may receive the happiness of Your saints in Your kingdom, through the grace, the compassion, and the love for men of Your only Son, with whom You are blessed, together with Your most holy, good, and life-giving Spirit, now and forever. Amen.

A Prayer to Saint Antonino, Patron of Campagna, for Liberation from Evil Spirits

Omnipotent and merciful God, you have granted to the Blessed St. Antonino, abbot, a special power against the devils; grant us we pray, that through his merits and his prayers, we may be liberated from their pitfalls and thus reach eternal life. We ask you through our Lord Jesus Christ, your Son, who is God and lives and reigns with you in the unity of the Holy Spirit forever and ever. Amen.

An Ancient Prayer to St. Antonino

O glorious St. Antonino, who on earth had the grace to conquer the devil, allow me to overcome all the assaults of the evil enemy, so that free and healthy, and following your luminous example, I may ever love the Lord better.

A Prayer That Priests May Come to Know
How to Gain Authority over the Devil

Heavenly Father, we come before You to present to You all Your holy, consecrated priests. We ask You, in Your love, to pour out Your Holy Spirit upon them. You have given them authority over Satan and his demons. We ask You to fill them with a renewed awareness of this power. Fortify them and sustain them so that they can act in Your Holy Spirit, in the name of Jesus, in order to expel Satan and his demons when and wherever they meet. Grant them a new vision so that, in Your light, they can clearly see this evil influence in their own lives, in the lives of those they love, and in their community.

Lord Jesus, come to illuminate the heart, mind, and soul of every priest. Fill them with You, so that they may be touched by wisdom and discernment. Grant them the necessary graces and gifts to fight the battles against evil.

Dear Mother Mary, we come before you to ask you to intercede for all your priestly sons before the three Persons of the Most Blessed Trinity. Send your angels and saints to defend them, protect them, and intercede for them. In the name of Jesus, let us pray. Amen. Alleluia. Amen.

A Prayer for One's Own Liberation

Holy Father, omnipotent and merciful God, in the name of Jesus Christ and through the intercession of the Virgin Mary, send Your Holy Spirit upon me; may the Spirit of the Lord descend upon me, mold me, form me, fill me, hear me, use me, heal me, cast out from me all the forces of evil, annihilate them, destroy them, so that I may be well and do good. Cast out from me all the spells, sorcery, black magic, black masses, evil eye, ties, curses, diabolical infestation, diabolical possession, diabolical obsession, all that is evil; sin, envy, jealousy, perfidy, discord, impurity, infatuation; physical, psychic, moral, spiritual, and diabolic illnesses. Burn all of these evils in hell, so that they will never again touch me or any other creature in the world.

In the name of Jesus Christ our Savior, through the intercession of the Immaculate Virgin Mary, I order and command all unclean spirits, all the presences that molest me, to leave me immediately, to leave me definitely, and, chained by St. Michael the Archangel, by St. Gabriel, by St. Raphael, by my guardian angel, crushed under the heel of the Most Holy Immaculate Virgin, to go into the eternal abyss.

Give me, O Father, much faith, joy, health, peace, and all the graces that I need. Lord Jesus, may Your most Precious Blood be upon me. Amen.

A Prayer to Jesus the Liberator

Lord Jesus Christ, You are the friend and Redeemer of all men; in Your name, all find salvation, and at Your name, every knee is bent in heaven, on earth, and under the earth. I beg You that I may adore You as the one true God. Illuminate and visit my heart, distance from me all temptation, oppression, and snares of the enemy. Heal me from my sins and from all infirmity, so that, adhering to Your lovable and perfect will, I may obey with perseverance the teachings of the gospel and that I may be a worthy dwelling of the Holy Spirit. Amen.

An Act Denouncing Evil

I reject the evil that has infiltrated my life because I have distanced myself from Jesus; I have abandoned the mysteries, I have neglected prayer, and I have been devoted solely to what is passing. I refuse the evil that I have accepted and which I have stupidly committed through ignorance or thoughtlessness, through anger or unawareness, for fear of being considered different or of being criticized. I am aware of and reject whatever evil I have done and that I have caused all of society. In a special way, I reject the spiritually polluting actions of blasphemies, false promises and oaths, usury, the unjust delay of payments, injustices, favoritisms, séances, and all the occult practices. Christ, the Savior, save me by the power of Your Cross. Amen.

A Prayer against Sorcery
(From the Greek-Orthodox Ritual)

Kyrie eleison. God, our Lord, King of ages, all-powerful and almighty, You who made everything and who transforms everything simply by Your will; You who in Babylon changed into dew the seven-times-hotter furnace and protected and saved the three holy children; You are the doctor and physician of our souls. You are the salvation of those who turn to You. We beseech You to make powerless, banish, and drive out every diabolic power, presence, and machination; every evil influence, spell, or evil eye and all evil actions aimed against Your servants.

Where there is envy and malice, give us an abundance of goodness, endurance, victory, and charity. O Lord, You who love man, we beg You to reach out Your powerful hands and Your mighty arms and send the angel of peace over us, to protect us, body and soul. May he keep at bay and vanquish every evil power, every poison or malice invoked against us by corrupt and envious people. Then, under the protection of Your authority, may we sing in gratitude: The Lord is my salvation, whom shall I fear? I will not fear evil because You are with me, my God, my strength, my powerful Lord, Lord of peace, Father of all ages.

Yes, Lord our God, have compassion on Your image, and save Your servant [name] from every threat coming from the spell, and protect him by raising him above all evil. We ask You this through the intercession of our most blessed, glorious Lady, Mary ever Virgin, Mother of God, of the most splendid archangels, and all your saints. Amen.

A Prayer to the Blessed Virgin Mary

Mary, today I renew in your hands the promises of my baptism. I renounce forever Satan, the enemy of our joy. I renounce his deceits, his seductions, and all his works. I give myself entirely to Jesus, the living sign of God's love for us, in order to be more faithful to Him and in order to live fully as a child of God. I entrust myself to you, Immaculate Mary. I choose you as my Mother and Lady. To you, as your child, I abandon and consecrate my life, my family, and the community in which I live. I ever entrust myself to your wishes, O Mary; preserve me from sin and defend me from the Evil One. On the last day, receive me in your arms and present me to Jesus as your child. Then, singing the eternal song of praise to God, together with you, O merciful Mother, my paradise will begin and my soul will exult with joy. Amen.

A Prayer to Mary for Liberation
(St. Pius X)

August Queen of Heaven, sovereign Queen of Angels, you who at the beginning received from God the power and the mission to crush the head of Satan, we humbly beseech you, send your heavenly legions so that on your orders and by your powers they will track down demons, fight them everywhere, curb their audacity, and plunge them into the abyss. O divine Mother, send us your angels and archangels to defend us, to watch over us. Holy angels and archangels, defend us, protect us. Amen.

A Prayer to the Most Holy Trinity for Liberation
The blessing of the Most Holy Trinity (make the Sign of the Cross) with the protection of Mary Immaculate: accompany us throughout our life, give us strength and courage against the snares of Satan and his minions, raise us from every fall, heal us from every infirmity, give us strength and constancy in the way of goodness, give us peace, serenity, and love, and lead us into the paternal arms of God. Amen.

An Optional Prayer for the Fourth Sunday of Lent
Good and faithful God, who never tires of converting those who go astray: through Your Son, raised up on the Cross, heal us from the bites of the Evil One and grant us the richness of Your grace so that, renewed in spirit, we may return Your eternal and boundless love, through Christ our Lord. Amen.

An Invocation of the Blessed Virgin Mary against Diabolical Invasions
O Immaculate Virgin, Mother of God and our Mother, Queen of the Angels, accept my heartfelt supplications and present them before the throne of the Most High. Through your Divine Son, you have received from God the mission of crushing the proud head of Satan. Therefore, God has made you immaculate from your conception and filled you with grace. Thus, you can facilitate in us the redemptive action of Christ. We beg you now to obtain for us from God the sending of the holy angels, so that they may repel the demon tempters, reveal their deceits, repress their audacity, and send them back to hell. Help us, O loving

Mother, to become more humble in the presence of God and of men. Help us to become ever more decisive in pushing back the assaults of impurity and covetousness. Help us to be faithful and solicitous in prayer. Help us to grow in love for the Holy Mass and Holy Communion. Help us to love our neighbor, to live in peace with everyone, and to forgive offenses and misunderstandings, so that we may offer to the heart of your Jesus the joy of seeing His gospel message fulfilled. Under your mantle of mercy may we find refuge, O Holy Mother of God, certain of being defended from evil suggestions and from the infernal enemy, and keep us faithful in the paternal goodness of God. Let us be confident of entering the eternal joy of heaven in order to sing in eternity the divine mercy. Amen.

A Prayer against the Snares of the Devil
(St. Isidore of Seville, Prayer against Diabolical
Snares, PL 83, 1273-1276)

O Lord, you are the true Doctor and the true bearer of help; You are the Creator and the Redeemer, the Giver of gifts, the Donor, the Advocate, and the mighty and merciful Judge; You give light to the blind; You permit what You command to become possible for us, the infirm; You are so heartfelt in wanting us to pray fervently; You are so munificent in not permitting us to despair. O good Jesus, be merciful toward me, with all my sins and all my errors; with the act of Your gratuitous goodness, introduce me to that desirable contemplation where it is never possible to err. You who know all hidden things, You know well how many vices I have run up against. You know how miserable and vacillating I am; You know from which enemy I am continuously afflicted and assaulted. In my struggles I search for You, O Christ, strong, triumphant and ever-victorious leader. If the furious lion

is overcome by the infirm sheep, if the most violent spirit is conquered by the weakest flesh, and if also for some time we suffer,
permitted by one of Your just judgments, You do not ever allow
the demon's dominion to swallow us with his insatiable jaws.
O Lover of men, to the Evil One that exults over our failures,
restrict the sadness that competes with our human joy. Amen.

An Invocation of the Virgin against Satan

O Mary, Holy Virgin, immaculate and pure, look at your children humbly prostrated before you. The ancient serpent, against
whom the first divine curse was hurled, continues to fight, to
undermine, and to tempt us children of Eve. Mother, you crushed
his head from the first moment of your Immaculate Conception.
Help us, O Mary, in this struggle. Keep away from us the pitfalls
of the Evil One and the evil arts of his intermediaries. Let him
not triumph over our weakness. Rather, teach us to imitate your
virtues. Make us humble, full of faith, lofty and rich in grace, as
you were. Thus, we shall be strong against Satan, crush his head,
and be guided to that life where we will forever contemplate
Jesus, the blessed fruit of your womb, O clement, O pious, O
sweet Virgin Mary! Amen.

A Prayer against Every Evil

Spirit of our God, Father, Son, and Holy Spirit, Most Holy Trinity, Immaculate Virgin Mary, angels, archangels, and saints of
heaven, descend upon me. Please purify me, Lord, mold me, fill
me with Yourself, and use me. Banish all evil powers from me,
destroy them, remove them, so that I can be healthy and do good
deeds. Banish from me all spells, witchcraft, black magic, evil
deeds, ties, maledictions, and the evil eye; diabolic infestations,
oppressions, and possessions; all that is evil, sinful, and jealous:

perfidy, envy, and physical, psychological, moral, spiritual, and diabolical ailments. Burn all these evils in hell, so that they may never again touch me or any other creature in the entire world. I command and bid all the power that molests me — by the power of God all-powerful, in the name of Jesus Christ our Savior through the intercession of the Immaculate Virgin Mary — to leave me forever, and to be consigned into everlasting hell, where they will be bound by St. Michael the Archangel, St. Gabriel, St. Raphael, and our guardian angels and where they will be crushed under the heel of the Immaculate Virgin Mary. Amen.

A Prayer of Liberation
(Father Emiliano Tardif)

O Jesus, my Savior, my Lord and my God, my everything, who with the sacrifice of the Cross have redeemed us and defeated the power of Satan, I beg You to deliver me from every harmful presence and influence of the Evil One. I ask You in Your name, and I ask You in Your wounds; I ask You in Your blood, and I ask You in Your Cross. I ask You through the intercession of Mary, immaculate and sorrowful. May the blood and the water that flows from Your side descend upon me, purify me, liberate me, and heal me. Amen.

St. Alphonsus's Prayer of Liberation
(Personal Exorcism)

In the name of the Most Holy Trinity, Father, Son and Holy Spirit: Get you hence, Satan! By the merits of the Most Precious Blood of Jesus, by the intercession of the Immaculate Heart of Mary, of St. Joseph, and of all the saints, of St. Michael and all the angels! Amen.

About the Authors

Father Amorth

Gabriele Amorth, the most famous Italian exorcist and Mariologist, was born in Modena, Italy, on May 1, 1925. He served in the military during World War II. After the war, he received his degree in jurisprudence and served as the chief assistant to Giulio Andreotti, helping him in the formation of Italy's postwar government and the writing of its constitution. He entered the Society of St. Paul and was ordained a priest in 1954. In 1985, he was nominated as an exorcist of the Diocese of Rome, a ministry he practiced until his death.

As a Pauline, Father Amorth spoke about his ministry in the mass media, educating the faithful and Churchmen on the existence of the devil and his evil actions in the world. In 1990, he founded the International Association of Exorcists, of which he was president until 2000. He wrote more than thirty books, which have been translated into numerous languages.

May the Lord receive him in glory!

Father Stanzione

Don Marcello Stanzione, a priest, pastor, angelologist, and author of more than two hundred books on ecology and spirituality, was born in Salerno (Campania) in 1963. In 2002, he refounded the Militia of St. Michael the Archangel (http://www.miliziadisan-michelearcangelo.org/) in order to spread devotion to the holy angels and their prince, St. Michael: man's guardian in the battle against the devil. Each Michaelmas, in Rome, the Militia holds a three-day national meeting on the angels. *The Ecology and the Angelic World* was presented by Don Marcello Stanzione at the national meeting in 2018.

Sophia Institute

Sophia Institute is a nonprofit institution that seeks to nurture the spiritual, moral, and cultural life of souls and to spread the Gospel of Christ in conformity with the authentic teachings of the Roman Catholic Church.

Sophia Institute Press fulfills this mission by offering translations, reprints, and new publications that afford readers a rich source of the enduring wisdom of mankind.

Sophia Institute also operates the popular online resource CatholicExchange.com. *Catholic Exchange* provides world news from a Catholic perspective as well as daily devotionals and articles that will help readers to grow in holiness and live a life consistent with the teachings of the Church.

In 2013, Sophia Institute launched Sophia Institute for Teachers to renew and rebuild Catholic culture through service to Catholic education. With the goal of nurturing the spiritual, moral, and cultural life of souls, and an abiding respect for the role and work of teachers, we strive to provide materials and programs that are at once enlightening to the mind and ennobling to the heart; faithful and complete, as well as useful and practical.

Sophia Institute gratefully recognizes the Solidarity Association for preserving and encouraging the growth of our apostolate over the course of many years. Without their generous and timely support, this book would not be in your hands.

www.SophiaInstitute.com
www.CatholicExchange.com
www.SophiaInstituteforTeachers.org

Sophia Institute Press® is a registered trademark of Sophia Institute.
Sophia Institute is a tax-exempt institution as defined by the
Internal Revenue Code, Section 501(c)(3). Tax ID 22-2548708.